LICKETY-SPLIT
QUILTS

LICKETY-SPLIT QUILTS

Fast Projects from BIG Blocks

LAURIE BEVAN

Martingale®
& COMPANY

Credits

CEO: Daniel J. Martin
President: Nancy J. Martin
Publisher: Jane Hamada
Editorial Director: Mary V. Green
Managing Editor: Tina Cook
Technical Editor: Laurie Baker
Copy Editor: Liz McGehee
Design Director: Stan Green
Illustrator: Laurel Strand
Cover and Text Designer: Regina Girard
Photographer: Brent Kane

That Patchwork Place® is an imprint
of Martingale & Company®.

Lickety-Split Quilts:
Fast Projects from Big Blocks
© 2004 by Laurie Bevan

Martingale & Company
20205 144th Avenue NE
Woodinville, WA 98072-8478 USA
www.martingale-pub.com

Printed in China
09 08 07 06 05 04   8 7 6 5 4 3 2 1

Mission Statement

*Dedicated to providing quality products
and service to inspire creativity.*

Library of Congress Cataloging-in-Publication Data
Bevan, Laurie.
   Lickety-split quilts : fast projects from big blocks / Laurie Bevan.
      p. cm.
   Includes bibliographical references.
   ISBN 1-56477-551-8
   1. Patchwork—Patterns. 2. Quilting. I. Title.
   TT835.B384 2004
   746.46'041—dc22
                                          2004010492

Dedication

To my loving husband, Mike. Without him
I would not have my wonderful children,
Allan and Leigh, and without them all,
I would not be who I am.

Acknowledgments

To my dear friends, Suzanne Nelson, Laura Roberts,
and Suzanne Kolhagen. Thanks for your encouragement,
support, and sewing. I needed all three to write this book.

A great big thank you to all the women who quilted
the quilts in my book: Dawn, Janet, Laurie, Nicole, Pam,
and Virginia. I could not be more pleased.

I am grateful to Martingale & Company for turning
my idea into reality. You are not just my publisher,
you are all my friends.

Thank you to my editors, Laurie and Liz. Your talents
helped make my book the best it can be.

I want to thank Andover Fabrics for providing
wonderful fabrics for me to use in my designs.

Thank you, Cleo.

Contents

Introduction 10

The Big-Block Quilt 11

Projects

Dreaming of Flowers 14

Twilight Stars 19

Red-and-White Baskets 23

Green Tea 29

Springtime Sparkle 33

Flannel Fun 39

Hearts from the Past 45

Merry Christmas Wreath 50

Golden Autumn Wreath 55

Lightning Bug Lagoon 60

Whispering Windmills 65

For All My Sisters 69

Graphic Design 73

Quiltmaking Basics 79

Bibliography 93

About the Author 95

Introduction

Lickety-split means fast! Sometimes that's the kind of quilt we want to make, and many times that's the only quilt we have time to make.

A beautiful quilt does not have to be technically difficult or scrappy, or use hundreds of pieces, or take months to make. *Lickety-Split Quilts* has 13 fast, wonderful quilt projects. These quilts are fast to sew because they are made from big blocks, so you need fewer blocks to make a good-sized-quilt. None of the quilts in this book has more than 12 pieced blocks. All of the quilts are different; some are bold and exciting and some are soft and pretty, but all of them piece together quickly. Throughout this book, you'll find quilts in four sizes—wall, lap, twin, and double—to show that you can make any size quilt with the lickety-split method.

Twelve different blocks are presented. Two of the blocks are my own designs: Simple Basket and Sashed Hearts. Two of them were chosen for the book because they are favorites of mine: Sister's Choice and Friendship Star. For the other eight, I searched for blocks that were simple to piece, could be enlarged easily, and offered a new and different look. Take a glance at "Springtime Sparkle" on page 33. When was the last time you saw the Flying Bats block in a quilt? The resources I used in my search are listed in the bibliography on page 93.

One element of the lickety-split method is that each quilt is made using a limited number of fabrics. This simplifies the decision-making process. Several of my quilts were each made from fabrics chosen from just one "collection." A collection is a group of fabrics that coordinate and are from one designer. They often come in several different color groups. These collections, usually displayed together at quilt shops, allow you to easily choose three or four fabrics to make a quilt. "Hearts from the Past" on page 45, for example, is a quilt made entirely from one fabric collection. Many beginning quilters have not acquired a "stash" of fabric yet. Scrappy quilts are beautiful, but you wouldn't want to go and buy the number of fabrics it takes to make one. When you start by making your quilts from just a few fabrics, each time you finish a project, you have more pieces for your growing "stash."

Using a limited number of fabrics to make your quilt also speeds up the time you spend cutting and piecing. You will be cutting six strips from one fabric instead of one strip from six different fabrics. When you start sewing the pieces together for the blocks, each block uses the same fabric in the same position. This allows you to keep sewing; you don't have to stop and think, "Now where does this fabric go?"

For each quilt in the book, I have shown a color or fabric variation. This may help you to see past the one idea presented as the project quilt. Please don't dismiss a project you like simply because you don't care for the fabric colors. Think of the colors or fabrics you would use to make it, and give them a try.

Today's quilter lives in a hectic world in which there are too many quilts to make and not enough time to make them. The quilts in this book can be made in days, not months. If you are one of those busy quilters, *Lickety-Split Quilts* may be just the solution for you. I hope you find some time to quilt, and I hope you enjoy every minute of it!

The Big-Block Quilt

The best way to quickly make a quilt larger is to simply make the blocks bigger. Twelve 8" finished blocks set in four rows of three blocks each make your quilt center 24" x 32" finished. But twelve 16" finished blocks set in four rows of three blocks each make your quilt center 48" x 64" finished. You just grew from crib size to lap size and you didn't have to make any more blocks!

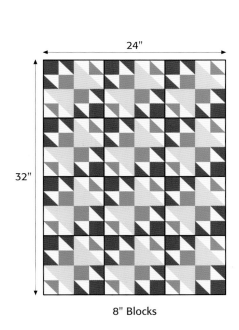

8" Blocks

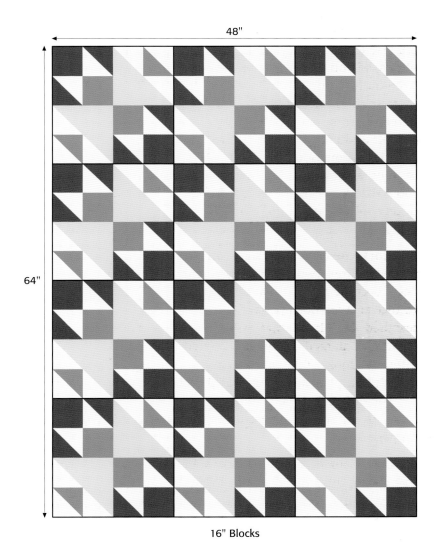

16" Blocks

Big Blocks

Many standard blocks can be enlarged to become big blocks. Choose simple blocks without too many pieces and ones that are made up of units that can be sewn with easy piecing techniques. Churn Dash, Ohio Star, and Pinwheel are good choices for big blocks. More complex blocks work well in a single big-block wall-hanging quilt, as you can see with the County Fair block that was used to make "Merry Christmas Wreath" on page 50. I made the finished block 20" x 20" so the many smaller pieces are still very simple to sew and you only have to make one block for a wall quilt that's the perfect size. Browse through the books listed in the bibliography on page 93 to find great blocks you can turn into big blocks for wonderful quilts.

To enlarge your block, follow these easy steps.

1. Choose your block and determine on which grid your block is built: two, three, four, or five. You can use a seven-grid block as well, like Bear's Paw, but because these blocks usually have quite a few pieces, they won't be as quick to assemble. The number of grid units should be the same across and down, and each grid unit should be the same size. The grid unit in each of these sample blocks is highlighted below. For example, if the Friendship Star block is 9" finished, then each grid unit is 3" x 3" finished.

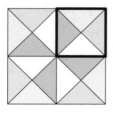

Electric Fan
2-Grid Block

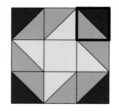

Friendship Star
3-Grid Block

Fireflies
4-Grid Block

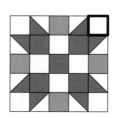

Sister's Choice
5-Grid Block

2. Once you know the grid size of your block, you can enlarge it to any size you want. Choose how big you want each finished grid unit to be and multiply that by the grid number to equal the finished size of your block. Using the previous blocks as examples, you can see how this works.

Electric Fan: Each grid unit will finish to 8"; it is a two-grid block.
8 x 2 = 16" finished block

Friendship Star: Each grid unit will finish to 5"; it is a three-grid block.
5 x 3 = 15" finished block

Fireflies: Each grid unit will finish to 4"; it is a four-grid block.
4 x 4 = 16" finished block

Sister's Choice: Each grid unit will finish to 3"; it is a five-grid block.
3 x 5 = 15" finished block

Sister's Choice would also be a great one-block quilt. If you make each grid unit finish to 4", the finished block will be 20". Add a border or two in her favorite colors, and you have a great one-block wall hanging to give as a gift to a sister or sister-in-law.

3. Cut and sew the grid units so they will finish to the size you have chosen.

You can have a lot of fun creating big blocks. Please don't let the math intimidate you; it's really quite easy.

Big Quilts

Once your big blocks are made, it's time to sew them into a big quilt. Now you have a decision to make. How big do you want your quilt to be?

If you arrange 12 blocks that are 15" square into a straight set of four rows of three blocks each, your finished quilt center will measure 45" x 60". But, if you set those same 12 blocks on point with alternate fabric squares and side and corner triangles, your finished quilt center will measure 63¾" x 85". With very little extra work, you've made your quilt 25" longer and almost 20" wider. Refer to "Calculating Corner and Side Triangles" on page 74 of *Sensational Settings: Over 80 Ways to Arrange Your Quilt Blocks, Revised Edition* by Joan Hanson (Martingale & Company, 2004) when designing your own on-point lickety-split quilts.

Borders will also add to the size of your quilt. With the lickety-split method, you can add large borders of beautiful fabrics. The quilts in this book use several different border treatments, each chosen to enhance the design of the quilt. There is the standard treatment: small inner border and large outer border, as I used in "Graphic Design" on page 73. Take a look at "Twilight Stars" on page 19. In this treatment the blocks seem to float because the large border is the same fabric as the block background. Maybe you don't need or want your quilt to be any larger. If so, don't add any borders, and after you quilt it, finish it off with the binding as I did with "Red-and-White Baskets" on page 23. Be careful not to overdo it. A border that is too large in proportion to the center of the quilt will not enhance your quilt design; it will just look as if you were trying to make your quilt bigger.

I hope you will feel inspired to design your own lickety-split quilt very soon. Just think, once you start sewing, you're almost done!

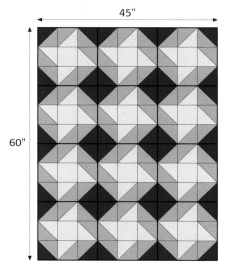

Straight Set

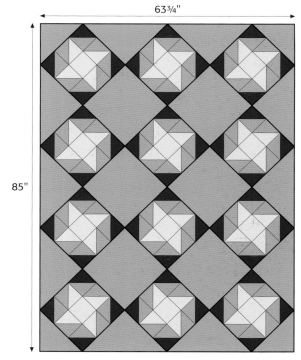

On Point

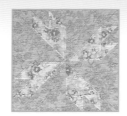

Dreaming of Flowers

I fell in love with this beautiful pink floral fabric and knew I had to use it in a quilt for myself. Even though the flowers in the print are not roses, I've always liked the Rosebud block and wanted to float the blocks on the perfect green background. This quilt is so soft and pretty, I just had to have it hand quilted.

Materials

Yardages are based on 42"-wide fabric.

3½ yards of pink floral for blocks, third border, and binding

3 yards of green tone-on-tone for blocks and first border

⅜ yard of dark pink for second border

5 yards of fabric for backing

71" x 86" piece of batting

Cutting

All cutting dimensions include ¼" seam allowances. Instructions are for cutting strips across the fabric width unless otherwise specified.

From the green tone-on-tone, cut:

6 strips, 8⅜" x 42"; crosscut into 24 squares, 8⅜" x 8⅜". Cut each square once diagonally to yield 48 triangles.

7 strips, 3⅜" x 42"; crosscut into 72 squares, 3⅜" x 3⅜". Cut 24 squares once diagonally to yield 48 triangles.

6 strips, 3½" x 42"

From the pink floral, cut:

4 strips, 5⅞" x 42"; crosscut into 24 squares, 5⅞" x 5⅞". Cut each square once diagonally to yield 48 triangles.

5 strips, 3⅜" x 42"; crosscut into 48 squares, 3⅜" x 3⅜"

From the *lengthwise* grain of the remaining pink floral, cut:

4 strips, 7½" wide

4 binding strips, 2½" wide

From the dark pink, cut:

6 strips, 1¼" x 42"

Block Assembly

1. Draw a diagonal line on the wrong side of the 48 green 3⅜" squares. Place each square right sides together with a pink floral 3⅜" square. Sew ¼" from each side of the drawn line. Cut the squares apart on the line and press the seams toward the floral triangles.

Make 96.

By Laurie Bevan. Quilted by Virginia Lauth, Shoreline, Washington.

Quilt Size: 67" x 82" • **Block Size:** 15" • **Block Name:** Rosebud

2. Sew the triangle squares from step 1 into pairs as shown. Make sure the colors are in the proper position. Press the seams in the direction shown.

3. Sew a green 3⅜" triangle to the floral end of each pair you made in step 2 as shown. Press the seams toward the triangle.

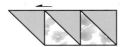

4. Sew a floral 5⅞" triangle to each unit from step 3 as shown. Press the seams toward the triangle.

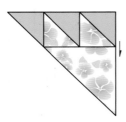

5. Sew a green 8⅜" triangle to each unit from step 4 along the diagonal edge as shown. Place the pieced unit on top so you can see the point of the rosebud petal when you sew. Press the seams toward the green triangle.

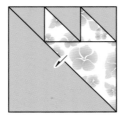

Make 48.

6. Sew the pieced units from step 5 together in pairs as shown. Press the seams in the direction indicated. Sew two of these units together to make each block, taking care to orient the units correctly. Press the seams in either direction.

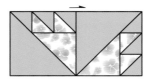

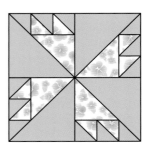

Make 12.

Quilt Assembly

1. Lay out the blocks in four horizontal rows of three blocks each as shown. If you rotate every other block 90°, you will have opposing seams at the block intersections. Sew the blocks into rows and press the seams in opposite directions from row to row. Sew the rows together and press the seams in one direction.

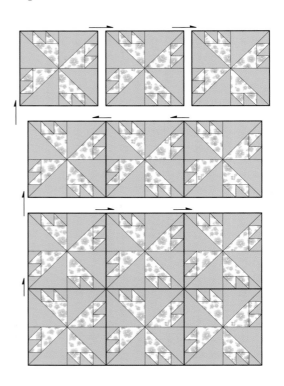

2. Refer to "Borders with Straight-Cut Corners" on page 85 before adding the borders to your quilt. Join three of the 3½"-wide green strips end to end. Repeat with the remaining three strips. From *each* long strip, cut one side border 60½" long and one top/bottom border 51½" long.

3. Sew the side borders to the quilt top and press the seams toward the borders. Sew the top and bottom borders to the quilt top and press the seams toward the borders.

4. Join the 1¼"-wide dark pink strips as in step 2. From *each* long strip, cut one side border 66½" long and one top/bottom border 53" long. Sew these border strips to the quilt top as in step 3.

5. Trim two of the 7½"-wide floral strips to 68" long for the side borders. Trim the remaining floral strips to 67" for the top and bottom borders. Sew these border strips to the quilt top as in step 3.

Finishing

1. If you plan to have your quilt professionally machine quilted, refer to "Professional Quilting" on page 88 before continuing this section.

2. Cut the backing fabric into two equal lengths, remove the selvages, and sew the two pieces together along the length to make a backing with a vertical seam. Press the seam to one side. Your backing should be at least 71" wide and 86" long.

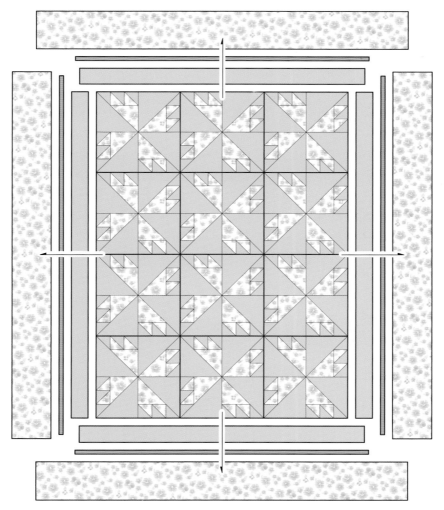

Quilt Assembly Diagram

3. Mark the quilt top if necessary. Layer the top with the batting and backing and baste the layers together using your preferred method (refer to "Preparing to Quilt" on page 87).

4. Hand or machine quilt as desired (refer to "Quilting Techniques" on page 87). This quilt was hand quilted. The rosebuds in the blocks were individually outline quilted and the block background was filled with small flowers. The green border was quilted with a small vine that has leaves and flowers. The narrow pink border was quilted in the ditch, and the floral border was quilted with a large vine and lots of leaves.

5. Remove any basting and trim the excess batting and backing fabric even with the edges of the quilt top. Join the four 2½"-wide floral strips end to end with diagonal seams and bind the quilt (refer to "Binding" on page 89).

6. Make a label for your quilt that includes your name, the city and state where you live, the date, and any other interesting information, and stitch it to the back of your quilt.

Midnight in the Garden

The project quilt may be soft and pretty, but with different fabrics you can easily sew up something dark and dramatic. Imagine decorating a bedroom using a quilt made with the fabrics in this block as the focal point and accenting it with wonderful accessory pieces in reds and blacks.

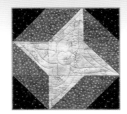

Twilight Stars

The Friendship Star is one of my favorite blocks. Maybe that's because of the name. I've made so many dear friends since I started quilting—friends who have taught me, shared with me, and listened to me. I've always wanted to use this block in a quilt with fabrics the colors of the sky at twilight. At this time of day, the stars are just beginning to show themselves—like friends you make, one by one.

Materials

Yardages are based on 42"-wide fabric.

2⅛ yards of dark blue print for blocks and border

2⅛ yards of medium blue print for blocks and binding

1⅛ yards of light blue print for blocks

3¾ yards of fabric for backing

62" x 77" piece of batting

Cutting

All cutting dimensions include ¼" seam allowances. Instructions are for cutting strips across the fabric width unless otherwise specified.

From the medium blue print, cut:
8 strips, 5⅞" x 42"; crosscut into 48 squares, 5⅞" x 5⅞"
7 binding strips, 2½" x 42"

From the light blue print, cut:
4 strips, 5⅞" x 42"; crosscut into 24 squares, 5⅞" x 5⅞"
2 strips, 5½" x 42"; crosscut into 12 squares, 5½" x 5½"

From the *lengthwise* grain of the dark blue print, cut:
4 strips, 6½" wide
2 strips, 5⅞" wide; crosscut into 24 squares, 5⅞" x 5⅞"

Block Assembly

1. Draw a diagonal line on the wrong side of each medium blue square. Place the squares right sides together with each light and dark blue 5⅞" square. Sew ¼" from each side of the drawn line. Cut the squares apart on the line and press the seams toward the medium blue triangles.

Make 48.   Make 48.

By Laurie Bevan. Quilted by Laurie Jarmer, Tualatin, Oregon.

Quilt Size: 57½" x 72½" • **Block Size:** 15" • **Block Name:** Friendship Star

2. To make each block, arrange four light blue/ medium blue triangle squares, four dark blue/ medium blue triangle squares, and one light blue 5½" square into three horizontal rows as shown. Sew the units in each row together. Press the seams in the directions indicated. Sew the rows together. Press the seams toward the center row.

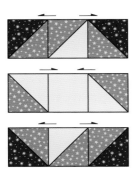

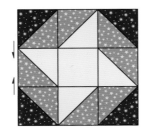

Make 12.

Quilt Assembly

1. Lay out the blocks in four horizontal rows of three blocks each as shown. If you rotate every other block 90°, you will have opposing seams at the block intersections. Sew the blocks into rows and press the seams in opposite directions from row to row. Sew the rows together and press the seams in one direction.

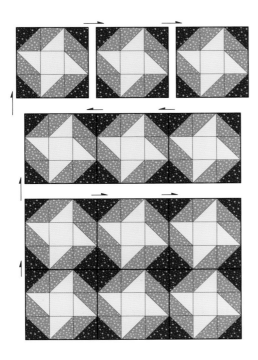

2. Refer to "Borders with Straight-Cut Corners" on page 85 before adding the borders to your quilt. Trim two of the 6½"-wide dark blue strips to 60½" long. Sew them to the sides of the quilt top and press the seams toward the borders.

3. Trim the remaining two dark blue strips to 57½" long. Sew them to the top and bottom of the quilt top and press the seams toward the borders.

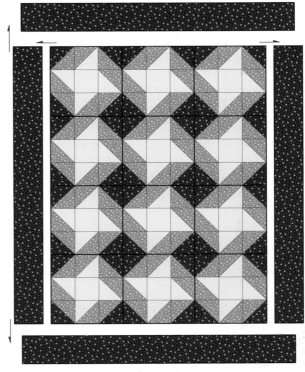

Quilt Assembly Diagram

Finishing

1. If you plan to have your quilt professionally machine quilted, refer to "Professional Quilting" on page 88 before continuing this section.

2. Cut the backing fabric into two equal lengths, remove the selvages, and sew the two pieces together along the length to make a backing with a horizontal seam. Press the seam to one side. Your backing should be at least 62" wide and 77" long.

3. Mark the quilt top if necessary. Layer the top with the batting and backing and baste the layers together using your preferred method (refer to "Preparing to Quilt" on page 87).

4. Hand or machine quilt as desired (refer to "Quilting Techniques" on page 87). This quilt was professionally machine quilted with a large flower shape inside the stars, lots of swirling curves in the background, and a star in the center of the dark blue sections. The border was quilted with larger, interlocking curves, with a star in each corner.

5. Remove any basting and trim the excess batting and backing even with the edges of the quilt top. Join the seven 2½"-wide medium blue strips end to end with diagonal seams and bind the quilt (refer to "Binding" on page 89).

6. Make a label for your quilt that includes your name, the city and state where you live, the date, and any other interesting information, and stitch it to the back of your quilt.

Stars and Stripes

Red, white, and blue fabrics make a wonderful color combination for the Friendship Star block. Use a red-and-white striped fabric on the corners of each block, and when you put four blocks together, the corners create a pinwheel design. This would be a great quilt for someone serving our country in the military.

Red-and-White Baskets

Back in 1995, before I learned how to appliqué, I wanted to make a basket-block quilt, but all the patterns I found had appliquéd handles. So I designed this basket block with a pieced handle and made a small wall quilt (see page 28 for a photograph.) I wanted to include my original block in this book, and these beautiful red-and-white fabrics make a very traditional two-color quilt without borders; it is simply finished with binding. My good friend Suzanne Kolhagen sent me pieces of these fabrics because she liked them and knew I would like them, too. Well, I liked them so much I purchased a bunch more and sent them back to Suzanne, who did a wonderful job piecing this quilt top for my book. Suzanne, I'll be sending this quilt back to you for your collection.

Materials

Yardages are based on 42"-wide fabric.

5⅜ yards of white-with-red print for pieced block background, alternate blocks, and setting triangles

1¾ yards of red plaid for baskets

¾ yard of red-and-white floral for basket flowers*

¾ yard of red-with-white print for binding

5½ yards of fabric for backing

72" x 95" piece of batting

Template plastic (optional)

* *Purchase 1 yard if you wish to fussy cut the floral triangles; see page 25.*

Cutting

All cutting dimensions include ¼" seam allowances. Instructions are for cutting strips across the fabric width unless otherwise specified.

From the red plaid, cut:
2 strips, 11⅝" x 42"; crosscut into 6 squares, 11⅝" x 11⅝". Cut each square once diagonally to yield 12 triangles.
8 strips, 1½" x 42"; crosscut into:
  • 12 strips, 1½" x 11"
  • 12 strips, 1½" x 12"
2 strips, 4½" x 42"; crosscut into 12 squares, 4½" x 4½"
2 strips, 4⅛" x 42"; crosscut into 12 squares, 4⅛" x 4⅛". Cut each square once diagonally to yield 24 triangles.

From the red-and-white floral, cut:
6 squares, 9⅝" x 9⅝"; cut each square once diagonally to yield 12 triangles

Designed by Laurie Bevan. Pieced by Suzanne Kolhagen, Key West, Florida. Quilted by Dawn Kelly, Sagle, Idaho.

Quilt Size: 68⅜" x 91" • **Block Size:** 16" • **Block Name:** Simple Basket

Fussy Cutting

To get the best bouquets of flowers for the baskets in this quilt, the floral triangles were fussy cut using a plastic triangle template. To do this, draw a 9⅝" square on a piece of template plastic and draw a diagonal line through the center of the square to make two triangles. Cut out one of the triangles along the lines. You will need more fabric for this technique than what is required in the materials list. A one-yard piece should give you plenty of designs to choose from. You can see through the plastic template, so place it anywhere you like on your fabric and cut out that piece for your quilt. When you're done cutting all of the triangles, you'll end up with a leftover scrap of fabric that looks like Swiss cheese. To see an example of triangles that were cut from 9⅝" squares as in the cutting instructions, look at the block variation on page 28.

From the white-with-red print, cut:

Note: To get the most out of your fabric, follow these cutting instructions exactly.

3 strips, 24" x 42"; crosscut *2 strips each* into:
- 1 square (2 total), 24" x 24"; cut the square twice diagonally to yield 4 (8 total) side triangles
- 1 square (2 total), 12½" x 12½"; cut the square once diagonally to yield 2 (4 total) corner triangles

Crosscut the *remaining strip* into:
- 1 square, 24" x 24"; cut the square twice diagonally to yield 4 side triangles. You will use 2 triangles and have 2 left over.
- 1 square, 7⅜" x 7⅜"; cut the square once diagonally to yield 2 triangles

3 strips, 16½" x 42"; crosscut into 6 squares, 16½" x 16½"

1 strip, 7⅜" x 42"; crosscut into 5 squares, 7⅜" x 7⅜". Cut each square once diagonally to yield 10 triangles.

6 strips, 3¾" x 42"; crosscut into 24 rectangles, 3¾" x 10"

8 strips, 2½" x 42"; crosscut into:
- 12 rectangles, 2½" x 11¼"
- 12 rectangles 2½" x 13¼"

1 strip, 3" x 42"; crosscut into 12 squares, 3" x 3"

From the red-with-white print, cut:

9 strips, 2½" x 42"

Block Assembly

1. With right sides together, position an 11"-long plaid strip on the left edge of each floral triangle as shown, aligning one end of the strip with the 90° corner. The opposite end of the strip will extend slightly beyond the triangle. Sew the strip in place and press the seam toward the strip. Sew a 12"-long plaid strip to the top edge as shown, aligning one end of the strip with the first strip. Press the seam toward the strip. Trim the excess length of the strips even with the diagonal edge of the triangles.

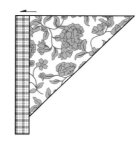
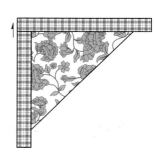

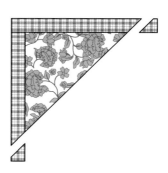

2. Draw a diagonal line on the wrong side of each 4½" plaid square. Align one square with the corner of each unit from step 1 as shown. Sew on the line. Trim the seam allowance to ¼" and press it toward the corner.

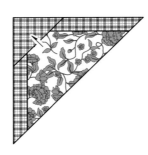

3. Draw a diagonal line on the wrong side of each 3" white-with-red print square. Align the square with the corner of each unit from step 2 as shown. Sew on the line. Trim the seam allowance to ¼" and press it toward the corner.

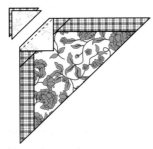

4. Sew an 11⅝" plaid triangle to the diagonal edge of each basket-top unit from step 3. Press the seams toward the basket bottom and trim any "dog ears." You will be sewing two long bias edges together. Be careful that they don't stretch!

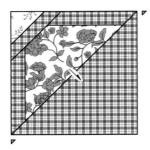

5. Sew a 2½" x 11¼" white-with-red print rectangle to the left edge of each basket unit and a 2½" x 13¼" white-with-red print rectangle to the top edge of each basket unit as shown. Press the seams toward the rectangles.

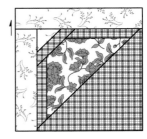

6. Sew a 4⅛" plaid triangle to one end of each 3¾" x 10" white-with-red rectangle, positioning the triangles as shown to make 12 of each strip. Press the seams toward the triangles.

 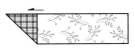

Make 12.   Make 12.

7. Sew the appropriate rectangle from step 6 to the bottom edge of each basket unit as shown and press the seam toward the rectangle. Sew the remaining rectangles to the right edge of each basket unit as shown and press the seam toward the rectangle.

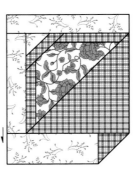

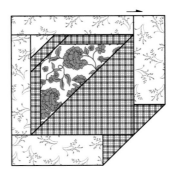

8. Fold each 7⅜" white-with-red print triangle in half along the long edge and finger press. With right sides together, center the crease with the bottom point of the basket. Sew the seam and press it toward the background triangle. Trim any "dog ears."

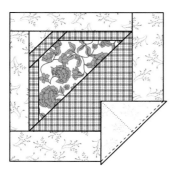

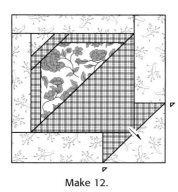

Make 12.

Quilt Assembly

1. Lay out the basket blocks, the 16½"-square white-with-red print alternate blocks, and the side and corner triangles in diagonal rows as shown.

2. Sew the blocks and side triangles in each row together and press the seams toward the alternate blocks and triangles. Sew the rows together and press the seams in either direction. Sew a corner triangle to each corner of the quilt top and press the seams toward the corners.

3. Refer to "Arranging On-Point Layouts" on page 84 to trim the edges of the quilt top, leaving a ¼" seam allowance beyond the block points. Square up the four corners.

Finishing

1. If you plan to have your quilt professionally machine quilted, refer to "Professional Quilting" on page 88 before continuing this section.

2. Cut the backing fabric into two equal lengths, remove the selvages, and sew the two pieces together along the length to make a backing with a vertical seam. Press the seam to one side. Your backing should be at least 72" wide and 95" long.

3. Mark the quilt top if necessary. Layer the top with the batting and backing and baste the layers together using your preferred method (refer to "Preparing to Quilt" on page 87).

4. Hand or machine quilt as desired (refer to "Quilting Techniques" on page 87). This quilt was professionally machine quilted with a large flower design on each of the baskets with flowers trailing up into the floral print. The baskets were outline quilted. The entire background was quilted with feather motifs.

5. Remove any basting and trim the excess ba ting and backing even with the edges of th quilt top. Join the nine red-with-white prir strips end to end with diagonal seams an bind the quilt (refer to "Binding" on page 89

6. Make a label for your quilt that includes you name, the city and state where you live, th date, and any other interesting informatior and stitch it to the back of your quilt.

Country Basket

The fabrics I used for this block variation are almost exactly like the ones I used for the blocks in the original wall quilt I made back in 1995 (shown at right). The colors still work for me!

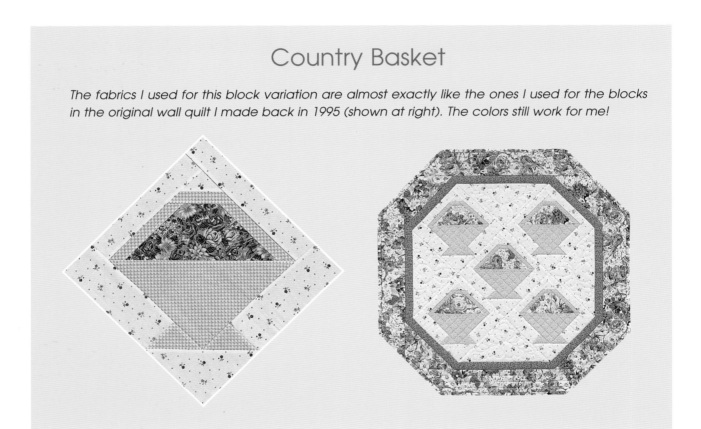

Green Tea

A wall quilt can be lickety-split, too. Just make a few blocks that are slightly larger than the average size, and in no time you will have a quilt top. To make this quilt look more "artsy," I turned one of the leaf blocks 90° from the others and used two different border fabrics in two different widths. The binding brings out the orange in the other fabrics and makes the fabrics sparkle.

Materials

Yardages are based on 42"-wide fabric.

¾ yard of medium green batik for blocks

⅝ yard of cream tone-on-tone for blocks

⅜ yard of dark green print for narrow border strips

⅜ yard of green floral for wide border strips

⅜ yard of dark orange print for binding

1⅜ yards of fabric for backing

40" x 40" piece of batting

Cutting

All cutting dimensions include ¼" seam allowances. Instructions are for cutting strips across the fabric width.

From the cream tone-on-tone, cut:
2 strips, 3⅞" x 42"; crosscut into 18 squares,
    3⅞" x 3⅞"
2 strips, 3½" x 42"; crosscut into 18 squares,
    3½" x 3½"

From the medium green batik, cut:
2 strips, 3⅞" x 42"; crosscut into 18 squares,
    3⅞" x 3⅞"
3 strips, 3½" x 42"; crosscut into 27 squares,
    3½" x 3½"

From the dark green print, cut:
2 strips, 3½" x 42"; crosscut into:
- 1 strip, 3½" x 27½"
- 1 strip, 3½" x 30½"

From the green floral, cut:
2 strips, 5" x 42"; crosscut into:
- 1 strip, 5" x 30½"
- 1 strip, 5" x 35"

From the dark orange print, cut:
4 strips, 2½" x 42"

Block Assembly

1. Draw a diagonal line on the wrong side of each cream 3⅞" square. Place each square right sides together with a medium green 3⅞" square. Sew ¼" from each side of the drawn line. Cut the squares apart on the line and press the seams toward the cream triangles.

Make 36.

By Laurie Bevan. Quilted by Dawn Kelly, Sagle, Idaho.

Quilt Size: 35" x 35" • **Block Size:** 9" • **Block Name:** Tea Leaf

2. To make each block, arrange four triangle squares from step 1, two cream 3½" squares, and three medium green 3½" squares into three horizontal rows as shown. Sew the units in each row together. Press the seams in the directions indicated. Sew the rows together. Press the seams in either direction.

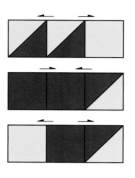
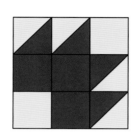

Make 9.

Quilt Assembly

1. Lay out the blocks in three horizontal rows of three blocks each as shown. Notice that the right-hand block in the second row is turned 90° to the left. Sew the blocks into rows and press the seams in opposite directions from row to row. Sew the rows together and press the seams toward the bottom of the leaf blocks.

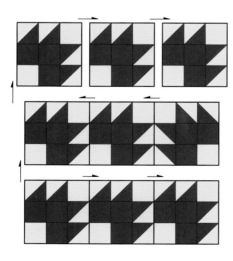

2. Refer to "Borders with Straight-Cut Corners" on page 85 before adding the borders to your quilt. Sew the dark green 3½" x 27½" strip to the left side of the quilt top and press the seam toward the border. Sew the dark green 3½" x 30½" strip to the top of the quilt top and press the seam toward the border.

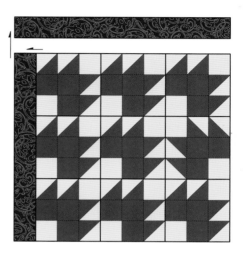

3. Sew the green floral 5" x 30½" strip to the right side of the quilt top and press the seam toward the border. Sew the green floral 5" x 35" strip to the bottom of the quilt top and press the seam toward the border.

Finishing

1. If you plan to have your quilt professionally machine quilted, refer to "Professional Quilting" on page 88 before continuing this section.

2. Cut the backing fabric into a 40" x 40" square.

3. Mark the quilt top if necessary. Layer the top with the batting and backing and baste the layers together using your preferred method (refer to "Preparing to Quilt" on page 87).

4. Hand or machine quilt as desired (refer to "Quilting Techniques" on page 87). This quilt was professionally machine quilted with bamboo branch motifs in the center of the quilt and an interlocking design in the borders.

5. Remove any basting and trim the excess batting and backing fabric even with the edges of the quilt top. Join the four orange strips end to end with diagonal seams and bind the quilt (refer to "Binding" on page 89).

6. Make a label for your quilt that includes your name, the city and state where you live, the date, and any other interesting information, and stitch it to the back of your quilt.

Falling Leaves

Use fabrics in rich tones of red, orange, gold, or brown to represent the gorgeous leaves of the fall season. If your fabric has a lot of variegated color, each leaf block will look slightly different, just like leaves in autumn.

Springtime Sparkle

I think this is a terrific block—easy to make, yet the design looks complex
when you put all the blocks together! Do you see the green and blue pinwheels
at the points where four blocks meet? I've always wanted to make a quilt using 1930s
reproduction fabric and a soft yellow background—and now I have.

Materials

Yardages are based on 42"-wide fabric.

5½ yards of light yellow solid for blocks, first
and third borders, and binding

⅜ yard of small-scale green print for blocks

⅜ yard of medium-scale green print for blocks

⅜ yard of small-scale blue print for blocks

⅜ yard of medium-scale blue print for blocks

½ yard of multicolored print for second border

5 yards of fabric for backing

71" x 87" piece of batting

Cutting

*All cutting dimensions include ¼" seam allowances.
Instructions are for cutting strips across the fabric
width unless otherwise specified.*

From the light yellow solid, cut:
3 strips, 8½" x 42"; crosscut into 12 squares,
8½" x 8½"
6 strips, 6½" x 42"; crosscut into 96 rectangles,
2½" x 6½"

12 strips, 2½" x 42"; crosscut into 192 squares,
2½" x 2½"
8 binding strips, 2½" x 42"

**From the *lengthwise* grain of the remaining
light yellow solid, cut:**
4 strips, 5½" wide
4 strips, 3½" wide

From the small-scale green print, cut:
4 strips, 2½" x 42"; crosscut into 24 rectangles,
2½" x 6½"

From the medium-scale green print, cut:
4 strips, 2½" x 42"; crosscut into 24 rectangles,
2½" x 6½"

From the small-scale blue print, cut:
4 strips, 2½" x 42"; crosscut into 24 rectangles,
2½" x 6½"

From the medium-scale blue print, cut:
4 strips, 2½" x 42"; crosscut into 24 rectangles,
2½" x 6½"

From the multicolored print, cut:
7 strips, 1½" x 42"

By Laurie Bevan. Quilted by Pam Clarke, Spokane, Washington.

Quilt Size: 66½" x 82½" • **Block Size:** 16" • **Block Name:** Flying Bats

Block Assembly

1. Draw a diagonal line on the wrong side of each yellow 2½" square. With right sides together, place a marked square at the left end of every blue and green rectangle as shown and sew on the diagonal line. Trim ¼" from the stitched line and press the seam toward the corner. Repeat to sew a marked square to the opposite end of each rectangle as shown. Be sure the two seam lines are parallel.

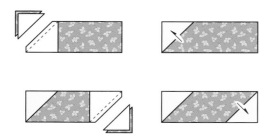

2. Sew a yellow rectangle to one side of each unit from step 1 as shown and press the seam toward the yellow rectangle.

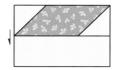

3. Sew pairs of units from step 2 together along the ends as shown. Be sure the fabrics in each pair are the same. Press the seam in either direction.

4. To make the blocks, sew a small-scale green print unit from step 3 to the top edge of each 8½" yellow square, stopping approximately 2" from the corner of the square as shown. There is no need to backstitch because you will be sewing over this stitching when you finish the block. Remove the block from the sewing machine and press the seam toward the rectangle.

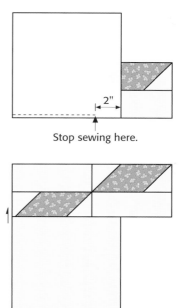

Stop sewing here.

5. Sew a medium-scale blue print unit from step 3 to the left edge of each square and press the seam toward the rectangle. Sew a medium-scale green print unit from step 3 to the bottom edge of each square and press the seam toward the rectangle.

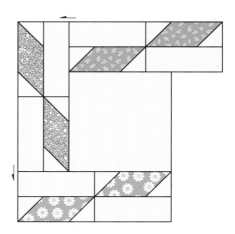

6. Fold back the unsewn end of the small-scale green print rectangle unit. Sew a small-scale blue print rectangle unit from step 3 to the right edge of each square and press the seam toward the rectangle.

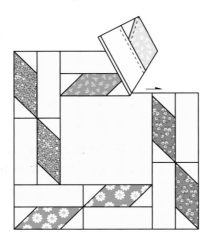

7. Finger-press the unsewn seam allowance of the small-scale green print rectangle unit flat and finish sewing this seam, starting ½" back into the first stitching and sewing to the end of the strip. Press the seam toward the rectangle.

Stop sewing here.   Start sewing here.

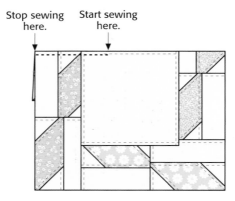

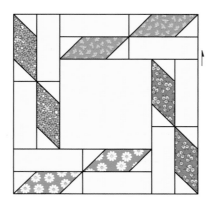

Quilt Assembly

1. Lay out the blocks in four horizontal rows of three blocks each as shown. Rotate the blocks so that the three blue pinwheels are made up of the same blue fabric and the three green pinwheels are made up of the two green fabrics. Sew the blocks into rows and press the seams in opposite directions from row to row. Sew the rows together and press the seams in one direction.

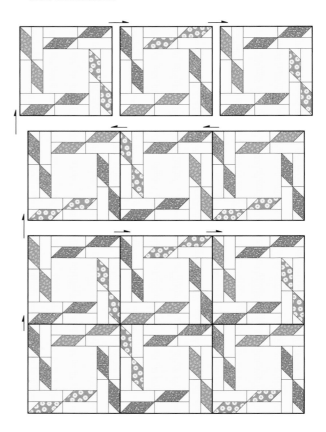

2. Refer to "Borders with Straight-Cut Corners" on page 85 before adding the borders to your quilt. Trim two of the 3½"-wide yellow strips to 64½" long. Sew these strips to the sides of the quilt top and press the seams toward the borders. Trim the remaining two 3½"-wide yellow strips to 54½" long. Sew these strips to the top and bottom of the quilt top and press the seams toward the borders.

3. Join two of the 1½"-wide multicolored strips end to end. Repeat with two more strips. From *each* long strip, cut one side border 70½" long. Sew these strips to the sides of the quilt top and press the seams toward the border. Join the remaining three multicolored strips end to end. From this long strip, cut two borders, each 56½" long. Sew these strips to the top and bottom edges of the quilt top and press the seams toward the borders.

4. Trim two of the 5½"-wide yellow strips to 72½" long for the side borders. Trim the remaining two 5½"-wide yellow strips to 66½" for the top and bottom borders. Sew these border strips to the quilt top as in step 2.

Finishing

1. If you plan to have your quilt professionally machine quilted, refer to "Professional Quilting" on page 88 before continuing this section.

2. Cut the backing fabric into two equal lengths, remove the selvages, and sew the two pieces together along the length to make a backing with a vertical seam. Press the seam to one side. Your backing should be at least 71" wide and 87" long.

3. Mark the quilt top if necessary. Layer the top with the batting and backing and baste the layers together using your preferred method (refer to "Preparing to Quilt" on page 87).

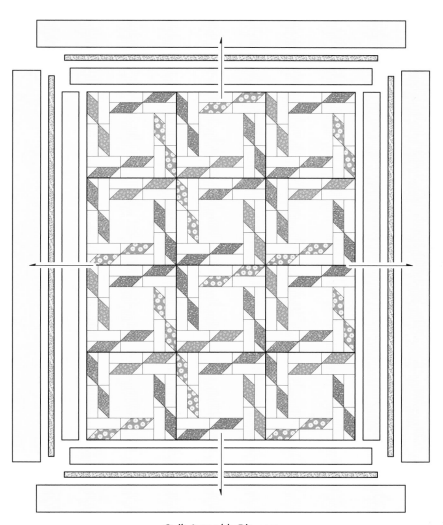

Quilt Assembly Diagram

4. Hand or machine quilt as desired (refer to "Quilting Techniques" on page 87). This quilt was professionally machine quilted. The blocks were covered with feathers and curlicues. The first border was stitched with feather motifs, the multicolored border with leaves on a vine, and the third border with swags, feathers, and curlicues.

5. Remove any basting and trim the excess batting and backing fabric even with the edges of the quilt top. Join the eight 2½"-wide yellow strips end to end with diagonal seams and bind the quilt (refer to "Binding" on page 89).

6. Make a label for your quilt that includes your name, the city and state where you live, the date, and any other interesting information, and stitch it to the back of your quilt.

Batty for Halloween

What a perfect fabric choice for the Flying Bats block! Use four blocks and a fun, spooky border print to make a great Halloween wall hanging.

Flannel Fun

Some quilters just love making flannel quilts, and my dear friend Suzanne is one of those quilters. She keeps trying to use up her stash of flannel fabric, but it just grows and grows. This flannel quilt was made with vibrant colors using the Bright Hopes block. To make it a little more interesting, three of the blocks are Four-Patch Bright Hopes blocks and these are placed randomly with the other nine blocks. The striped border with mitered corners is a fabulous finishing touch. This bright and cheerful quilt is a gift for Suzanne's daughter Amy. Happy snuggling!

Materials

Yardages are based on 42"-wide fabric.

2⅛ yards of striped flannel for border

1 yard of bright multicolored print flannel for block centers

¾ yard of magenta flannel for blocks

¾ yard of dark blue flannel for blocks

¾ yard of medium blue flannel for blocks

¾ yard of pink flannel for blocks

¾ yard of dark blue print flannel for binding

5 yards of fabric for backing

69" x 85" piece of batting

Cutting

All cutting dimensions include ¼" seam allowances. Instructions are for cutting strips across the fabric width.

From the bright print, cut:
3 strips, 8½" x 42"; crosscut into:
• 9 squares, 8½" x 8½"
• 4 squares, 4½" x 4½"
1 strip, 4½" x 42"; crosscut into 8 squares, 4½" x 4½"

From the magenta, cut:
3 strips, 4½" x 42"; crosscut into 9 rectangles, 4½" x 12½"
2 strips, 2½" x 42"; crosscut into 12 rectangles, 2½" x 6½"

From the dark blue for blocks, cut:
3 strips, 4½" x 42"; crosscut into 9 rectangles, 4½" x 12½"
2 strips, 2½" x 42"; crosscut into 12 rectangles, 2½" x 6½"

From the medium blue, cut:
3 strips, 4½" x 42"; crosscut into 9 rectangles, 4½" x 12½"
2 strips, 2½" x 42"; crosscut into 12 rectangles, 2½" x 6½"

From the pink, cut:
3 strips, 4½" x 42"; crosscut into 9 rectangles, 4½" x 12½"
2 strips, 2½" x 42"; crosscut into 12 rectangles, 2½" x 6½"

From the stripe, cut:
8 strips, 8½" x 42"

From the dark blue print, cut:
8 strips, 2¾" x 42"

Designed by Laurie Bevan. Pieced by Suzanne Nelson, Kenmore, Washington.
Quilted by Nicole Webb, Arlington, Washington.

Quilt Size: 64½" x 80½ " • **Block Size:** 16" • **Block Name:** Bright Hopes

Large Bright Hopes
Block Assembly

1. To make the blocks, sew a 4½" x 12½" magenta rectangle to the top edge of each 8½" bright-print square, stopping approximately 2" from the corner of the square as shown. There is no need to backstitch because you will be sewing over this stitching later. Remove the block from the machine and press the seam toward the rectangle.

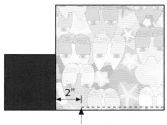

Stop sewing here.

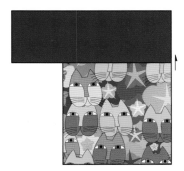

TIP

I often use a walking-foot attachment when I sew flannel quilts. Because the fabric is thicker and more loosely woven, the walking foot helps guide the fabric pieces evenly under the needle. This eliminates the problem of the top piece ending up longer than the bottom piece when you finish your seam. Try it!

2. Sew a 4½" x 12½" dark blue rectangle to the right edge of each bright-print square and press the seam toward the rectangle. Sew a 4½" x 12½" medium blue rectangle to the bottom edge of each square and press the seam toward the rectangle.

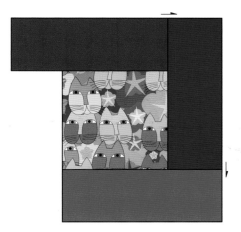

3. Fold back the unsewn end of the magenta rectangle. Sew a 4½" x 12½" pink rectangle to the left edge of each square and press the seam toward the rectangle.

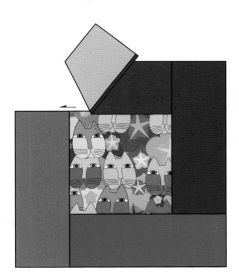

4. Finger-press the unsewn seam allowance of the magenta rectangle flat and finish sewing this seam, starting ½" back into the first stitching and sewing to the end of the strip. Press the seam toward the rectangle.

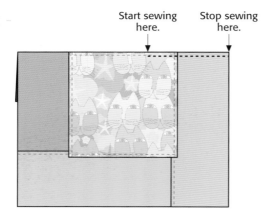

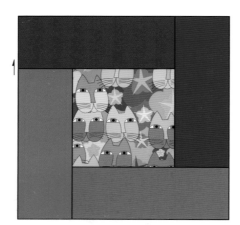

Make 9.

Four-Patch Bright Hopes Block Assembly

1. Using the 4½" bright-print squares and the 2½" x 6½" rectangles of the four colors, make 12 small Bright Hopes blocks, following the large Bright Hopes block instructions.

2. Sew four small Bright Hopes blocks together as shown to make the Four-Patch Bright Hopes blocks.

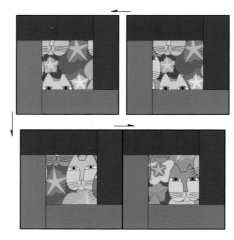

Make 3.

Quilt Assembly

1. Lay out the nine large and three Four-Patch Bright Hopes blocks in four horizontal rows as shown. Sew the blocks into rows and press the seams in opposite directions from row to row. Sew the rows together and press the seams in one direction.

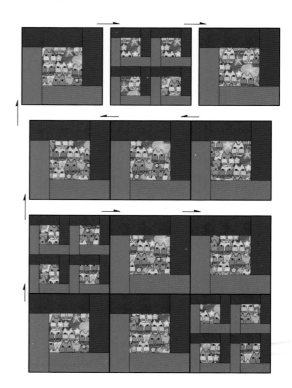

2. Join four of the striped strips together end to end to make a long strip. Repeat with the remaining four strips. From *each* of these long strips, cut one border strip 85" long and one border strip 69" long.

Note: When you use a striped fabric for the border, it's best to miter the corners so the stripes "continue" around the corner for a great finished look. To achieve this, the border strips are cut longer than the length of the quilt sides so there is enough fabric to make the mitered corners.

3. Refer to "Borders with Mitered Corners" on page 86 to attach the border strips to the quilt top.

Finishing

1. If you plan to have your quilt professionally machine quilted, refer to "Professional Quilting" on page 88 before continuing this section.

2. Cut the backing fabric into two equal lengths, remove the selvages, and sew the two pieces together along the length to make a backing with a vertical seam. Press the seam to one side. Your backing should be at least 69" wide and 85" long.

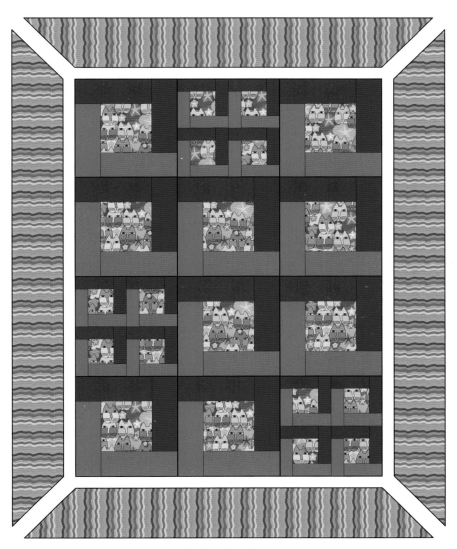

Quilt Assembly Diagram

3. Mark the quilt top if necessary. Layer the top with the batting and backing and baste the layers together using your preferred method (refer to "Preparing to Quilt" on page 87).

4. Hand or machine quilt as desired (refer to "Quilting Techniques" on page 87). This quilt was professionally machine quilted all over with a vine that has whimsical flowers and leaves.

5. Remove any basting and trim the excess batting and backing fabric even with the edges of the quilt top. Join the eight dark blue binding strips end to end with diagonal seams and bind the quilt (refer to "Binding" on page 89).

6. Make a label for your quilt that includes your name, the city and state where you live, the date, and any other interesting information, and stitch it to the back of your quilt.

Christmas Wonderland

Choose one or more great Christmas prints plus two red and two green fabrics and you have a quick Christmastime quilt. Make one for each of your guest beds to brighten up the holidays and make your visitors feel warm and welcome.

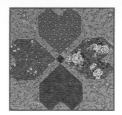

Hearts from the Past

Fabulous soft brown and pink floral fabrics give this simple Sashed Hearts block a stunning old-fashioned look. I love heart blocks, and I designed this one with four pieced hearts set with sashing and a center square. I set the blocks on point so there would be plenty of open space for beautiful quilting. There is a special room in my home waiting for this quilt.

Materials

Yardages are based on 42"-wide fabric.

4⅜ yards of brown-and-pink print for blocks, alternate blocks, and side and corner triangles

2⅞ yards of brown-and-pink floral for outer border and binding

¾ yard *each* of 4 different pink prints for blocks

½ yard of pink tone-on-tone for blocks and inner border

7 yards of fabric for backing

80" x 102" piece of batting

Cutting

All cutting dimensions include ¼" seam allowances. Instructions are for cutting strips across the fabric width unless otherwise specified.

From the brown-and-pink print, cut:
Note: To get the most out of your fabric, follow these cutting instructions exactly.

3 strips, 22½" x 42"; crosscut *each* strip into:
- 1 square (3 total), 22½" x 22½"; cut the square twice diagonally to yield 4 (12 total) side triangles. You will use 10 and have 2 left over.
- 1 square (3 total), 15½" x 15½"

2 strips, 15½" x 42"; crosscut into:
- 3 squares, 15½" x 15½"
- 2 squares, 11½" x 11½"; cut the squares in half once diagonally to yield 4 corner triangles

2 strips, 7½" x 42"; crosscut into 48 strips, 1½" x 7½"

4 strips, 3" x 42"; crosscut into 48 squares, 3" x 3"

6 strips, 2½" x 42"; crosscut into 96 squares, 2½" x 2½"

From *each* of the 4 pink prints, cut:
2 strips, 5" x 42"; crosscut into 12 squares, 5" x 5"

3 strips, 3" x 42"; crosscut into 24 rectangles, 3" x 5"

From the pink tone-on-tone, cut:
9 strips, 1½" x 42"; crosscut 1 strip into 2 pieces, 1½" x 20"; crosscut 1 of these pieces into 12 squares, 1½" x 1½"

From the *lengthwise* grain of the brown-and-pink floral, cut:
4 strips, 5½" wide
4 binding strips, 2½" wide

Block Assembly

1. Draw a diagonal line on the wrong side of each 2½" brown-and-pink print square. With right sides together, place a marked square on the lower left corner of 12 rectangles cut from

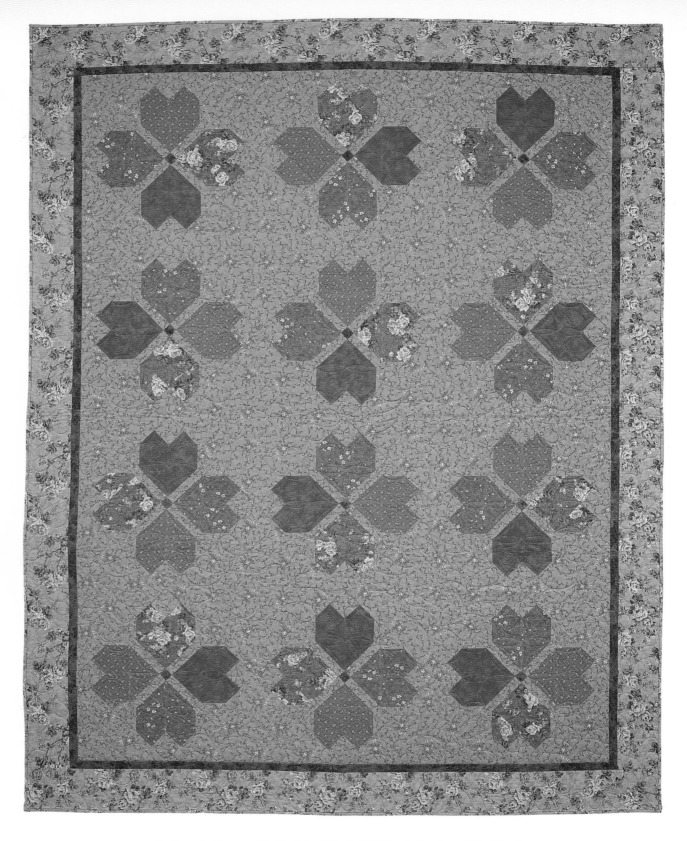

By Laurie Bevan. Quilted by Nicole Webb, Arlington, Washington.

Quilt Size: 76¼" x 97½" • **Block Size:** 15" • **Block Name:** Sashed Hearts

one of the four pink prints and the lower right corner of the remaining 12 rectangles of the same pink print, as shown. Sew on the diagonal line of each square, trim ¼" from the stitched line, and press the brown-and-pink triangle toward the corner. Repeat this step with the rectangles from the remaining three pink prints.

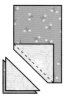 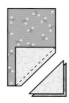

Left Unit   Right Unit

2. Sew each right unit from step 1 to a matching 5" pink square as shown. Press the seams toward the squares.

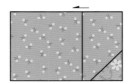

Right Heart Unit

3. Sew each left unit from step 1 to a 3" brown-and-pink print square as shown. Press the seams toward the squares.

Left Heart Unit

4. Sew each left heart unit to a right heart unit of the same pink print. Press the seam allowances toward the right heart units.

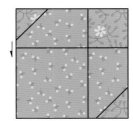

Make 12 of each print
(48 total).

5. To make each block, arrange four different heart units from step 4, four brown-and-pink 1½" x 7½" strips, and one 1½" pink tone-on-tone square into three horizontal rows as shown. Sew the pieces in each row together and press the seams in the directions indicated. Sew the rows together and press the seams toward the center row.

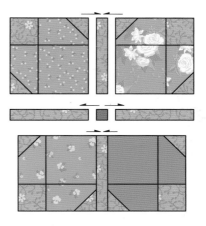

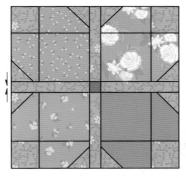

Make 12.

Quilt Assembly

1. Lay out the heart blocks, the 15½" square brown-and-pink print alternate blocks, and the side and corner triangles in diagonal rows as shown on page 48. Rotate the heart blocks to the left or right so different prints appear in different places in the blocks. This will give the quilt a scrappier look, even though all the hearts use the same four fabrics.

2. Sew the blocks and side triangles in each row together and press the seams toward the alternate blocks and triangles. Sew the rows together and press the seams in either direction. Sew a corner triangle to each corner of the quilt top and press the seams toward the corners.

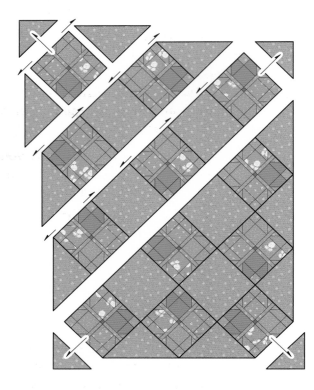

3. Refer to "Arranging On-Point Layouts" on page 84 to trim the edges of the quilt top, leaving a ¼" seam allowance beyond the block points. Square up the four corners.

4. Refer to "Borders with Straight-Cut Corners" on page 85 before adding the borders to your quilt. Cut the 20"-long pink tone-on-tone strip into two 10"-long pieces. Sew two 1½" x 42" pink tone-on-tone strips together end to end. Repeat with two additional 1½" x 42" pink tone-on-tone strips. Sew a 10" piece to one end of each of the long strips. Trim each of these strips to 85½" long. Sew one strip to each side of the quilt top and press the seams toward the borders.

5. Sew two of the remaining pink tone-on-tone strips together end to end. Repeat with the remaining two strips. Trim each of these strips to 66¼" long. Sew these strips to the top and bottom of the quilt top and press the seams toward the borders.

6. Trim two of the 5½"-wide brown-and-pink floral strips to 87½" long. Sew one strip to each side of the quilt top and press the seams toward the borders.

7. Trim the remaining two 5½"-wide brown-and-pink floral strips to 76¼" long. Sew these strips to the top and bottom of the quilt top and press the seams toward the borders.

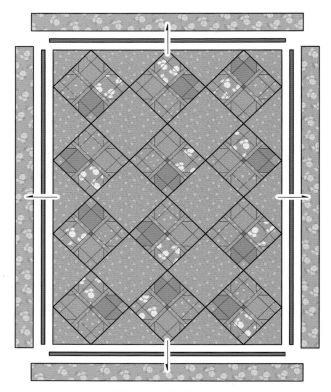

Quilt Assembly Diagram

Finishing

1. If you plan to have your quilt professionally machine quilted, refer to "Professional Quilting" on page 88 before continuing this section.

2. Cut the backing fabric into three equal lengths, remove the selvages, and sew the pieces together along the length to make a backing with two horizontal seams. Press the seams to one side. Your backing should be at least 80" wide and 102" long.

3. Mark the quilt top if necessary. Layer the top with the batting and backing and baste the layers together using your preferred method (refer to "Preparing to Quilt" on page 87).

4. Hand or machine quilt as desired (refer to "Quilting Techniques" on page 87). This quilt was professionally machine quilted using an original design on each of the hearts, with ribbons running between them in the sashing. The alternate blocks were quilted with large feathered wreaths, and feathers were quilted on the side and corner triangles as well. The inner border was quilted with more ribbons, and the floral border with more feathers.

5. Remove any basting and trim the excess batting and backing fabric even with the edges of the quilt top. Join the four 2½"-wide brown-and-pink floral strips end to end with diagonal seams and bind the quilt (refer to "Binding" on page 89).

6. Make a label for your quilt that includes your name, the city and state where you live, the date, and any other interesting information, and stitch it to the back of your quilt.

Valentine Hearts

Red and white fabrics turn the Sashed Heart block into a traditional two-color quilt. Use four different red fabrics for the hearts and a pretty white tone-on-tone fabric for the background. Your valentine will love the sweet combination.

Merry Christmas Wreath

This is the perfect Christmas wall hanging and would make a wonderful gift as well. The quilt is made from just one BIG block and a few glittering Christmas prints. The County Fair block is more complex than most blocks you would use for lickety-split quilts, but since you are making only one, and you are making it so big, a block with a lot of pieces makes a more interesting wall hanging.

Materials

Yardages are based on 42"-wide fabric.

⅝ yard of dark green print for block and binding

½ yard of Christmas floral for outer border

½ yard of gold print for block

⅜ yard of red print for block and inner border

¼ yard or fat eighth of holly print for block

¼ yard or fat eighth of pine print for block

1 yard of fabric for backing

32" x 32" piece of batting

Cutting

All cutting dimensions include ¼" seam allowances. Instructions are for cutting strips across the fabric width.

From the dark green print, cut:
4 squares, 2⅞" x 2⅞"; cut each square once diagonally to yield 8 triangles
2 strips, 2½" x 42"; crosscut into 24 squares, 2½" x 2½"
3 binding strips, 2½" x 42"

From the red print, cut:
4 squares, 2½" x 2½"
4 strips, 1" x 42"; crosscut into:
  • 2 strips, 1" x 20½"
  • 2 strips, 1" x 21½"

From the gold print, cut:
1 strip, 6½" x 42"; crosscut into:
  • 4 squares, 6½" x 6½"
  • 1 square, 6⅛" x 6⅛"
1 strip, 4½" x 42"; crosscut into 12 rectangles, 2½" x 4½"
1 strip, 2½" x 42"; crosscut into 8 squares, 2½" x 2½"

From the holly print, cut:
2 squares, 5½" x 5½"

From the pine print, cut:
2 squares, 5½" x 5½"

From the Christmas floral, cut:
4 strips, 3½" x 42"; crosscut into:
  • 2 strips, 3½" x 21½"
  • 2 strips, 3½" x 27½"

By Laurie Bevan. Quilted by Laurie Jarmer, Tualatin, Oregon.

Quilt Size: 27½" x 27½" • **Block Size:** 20" • **Block Name:** County Fair

Block Assembly

1. Sew a dark green triangle to two sides of each red square as shown. Press the seams toward the triangles.

Make 4.

2. Sew a triangle unit from step 1 to each side of the 6⅛" gold square. Press the seams toward the square.

3. Draw a diagonal line on the wrong side of each dark green square. With right sides together, place a square at one end of each gold rectangle. Sew on the diagonal line. Trim ¼" from the stitched line and press the seam toward the corner. Place another square at the opposite end of each rectangle. Be sure the diagonal line is oriented in the opposite direction of the first square. Sew, trim, and press as before.

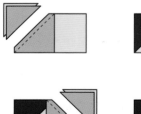

Make 12.

4. Place a holly-print square and a pine-print square right sides together. Draw two diagonal lines on the wrong side of one square as shown. Beginning at one corner, sew ¼" to the right of the line you're following until you reach the intersecting line. With your needle down on this line, turn the squares 90° and sew on the other diagonal line for ½". With your needle down, rotate the squares back 90° and continue sewing, now with your stitching ¼" to the left of the first line, until you reach the opposite corner. Remove the squares from your machine and sew the other diagonal line in the same manner. Cut along both diagonal lines and press each seam toward the holly print. Repeat this step with the other pair of holly and pine squares.

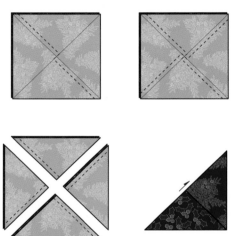

5. Sew two units from step 4 together as shown to make squares. Press the seams in either direction. Trim these squares to 4½" x 4½". Be sure to center your squares so you don't cut off any points.

Make 4.

6. Sew a unit from step 3 to the holly-print sides of each square from step 5 as shown. Be sure the dark green triangles are next to the

square. Press the seams toward the pieced squares.

7. Sew a 2½" gold square to each end of the remaining four units from step 3. Press the seams toward the squares.

8. Sew a unit from step 7 to the right side of a unit from step 6 as shown. Once again, be sure the dark green triangles are next to the pieced square. Press the seam toward the unit from step 7.

9. Arrange the four 6½" gold squares, the four units from step 8, and the center unit from step 2 as shown to make the block. Sew the units together into rows. Press the seams of the top and bottom rows toward the gold squares. Press the middle-row seams toward the center square. Sew the rows together to make the block. Press the seams toward the top and bottom rows.

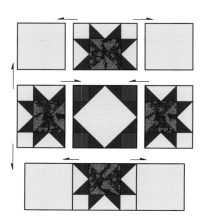

Quilt Assembly

1. Refer to "Borders with Straight-Cut Corners" on page 85 before adding the borders to your quilt. Sew a 1" x 20½" red strip to each side of the quilt top and press the seams toward the borders. Sew the 1" x 21½" red strips to the top and bottom of the quilt top and press the seams toward the borders.

2. Sew a 3½" x 21½" Christmas floral strip to each side of the quilt top and press the seams toward the borders. Sew the 3½" x 27½" Christmas floral strips to the top and bottom of the quilt top and press the seams toward the borders.

Quilt Assembly Diagram

Finishing

1. If you plan to have your quilt professionally machine quilted, refer to "Professional Quilting" on page 88 before continuing this section.

2. Cut the backing fabric into a 32" x 32" square.

3. Mark the quilt top if necessary. Layer the top with the batting and backing and baste the layers together using your preferred method (refer to "Preparing to Quilt" on page 87).

4. Hand or machine quilt as desired (refer to "Quilting Techniques" on page 87). This quilt was professionally machine quilted with large medallions of holly leaves and berries in the five gold squares. More holly leaves were quilted in the wreath and border, and more berries quilted in the red squares. The entire wreath and inner border were outline quilted.

5. Remove any basting and trim the excess batting and backing fabric even with the edges of the quilt top. Join the three 2½"-wide dark green strips end to end with diagonal seams and bind the quilt (refer to "Binding" on page 89).

6. Make a label for your quilt that includes your name, the city and state where you live, the date, and any other interesting information, and stitch it to the back of your quilt.

Snowflake

Turn the County Fair block into a sparkling snowflake. Use a wonderful snowflake print for the background that will accent the frosty center flake of this icy-cold winter wall hanging. Unlike the Christmas wreath quilt, the center square is cut from one of the snowflake fabrics, not the background.

Golden Autumn Wreath

Decorate your home for the fall season with this striking wall quilt or give it as a gift to a friend or relative with an autumn birthday. Thanks to Laura for taking my "Merry Christmas Wreath" (page 50) design into another season. Remember, for an interesting wall hanging, use a more complex block and make it a great-big one.

Materials

Yardages are based on 42"-wide fabric.

½ yard of autumn floral for outer border

¾ yard of black solid for block and binding

⅜ yard of gold batik for block

⅜ yard of orange tone-on-tone for block and inner border

¼ yard or fat eighth of orange floral for block

¼ yard or fat eighth of green leaf print for block

1 yard of fabric for backing

32" x 32" piece of batting

Cutting

All cutting dimensions include ¼" seam allowances. Instructions are for cutting strips across the fabric width.

From the gold batik, cut:
4 squares, 2⅞" x 2⅞"; cut each square once diagonally to yield 8 triangles
2 strips, 2½" x 42"; crosscut into 24 squares, 2½" x 2½"

From the orange tone-on-tone, cut:
4 squares, 2½" x 2½"
4 strips, 1" x 42"; crosscut into:
   • 2 strips, 1" x 20½"
   • 2 strips, 1" x 21½"

From the black solid, cut:
1 strip, 6½" x 42"; crosscut into:
   • 4 squares, 6½" x 6½"
   • 1 square, 6⅛" x 6⅛"
1 strip, 4½" x 42"; crosscut into 12 rectangles, 2½" x 4½"
1 strip, 2½" x 42"; crosscut into 8 squares, 2½" x 2½"
3 binding strips, 2½" x 42"

From the orange floral, cut:
2 squares, 5½" x 5½"

From the green leaf print, cut:
2 squares, 5½" x 5½"

From the autumn floral, cut:
4 strips, 3½" x 42"; crosscut into:
   • 2 strips, 3½" x 21½"
   • 2 strips, 3½" x 27½"

Designed by Laurie Bevan. Pieced by Laura Roberts, Lafayette, Colorado.
Quilted by Z. J. Humbach, Nederland, Colorado.

Quilt Size: 27½" x 27½" • **Block Size:** 20" • **Block Name:** County Fair

Block Assembly

1. Sew a gold triangle to two sides of each orange tone-on-tone square as shown. Press the seams toward the triangles.

Make 4.

2. Sew a triangle unit from step 1 to each side of the 6⅛" black square. Press the seams toward the square.

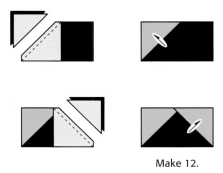

3. Draw a diagonal line on the wrong side of each gold square. With right sides together, place a square at one end of each black rectangle. Sew on the diagonal line. Trim ¼" from the stitched line and press the seam toward the corner. Place another square at the opposite end of each rectangle. Be sure the diagonal line is oriented in the opposite direction of the first square. Sew, trim, and press as before.

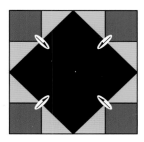

Make 12.

4. Place an orange floral square and a green leaf-print square right sides together. Draw two diagonal lines on the wrong side of one square as shown. Beginning at one corner, sew ¼" to the right of the line you're following until you reach the intersecting line. With your needle down on this other diagonal line, turn the squares 90° and sew on the other diagonal line for ½". With your needle down, turn the squares back 90° and continue sewing, now with your stitching ¼" to the left of the first line, until you reach the opposite corner. Remove the squares from your machine and sew the other diagonal line in the same manner. Cut along both diagonal lines and press each seam toward the orange floral. Repeat this step with the other pair of orange floral and green leaf-print squares.

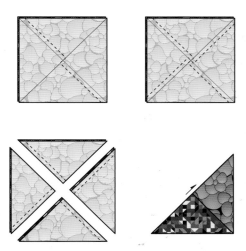

5. Sew two units from step 4 together as shown to make squares. Press the seams in either direction. Trim these squares to 4½" x 4½". Be sure to center your squares so you don't cut off any points.

Make 4.

6. Sew a unit from step 3 to the orange floral side of each square from step 5 as shown. Be

sure the gold triangles are next to the square. Press the seams toward the pieced squares.

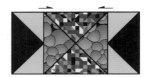

7. Sew a 2½" black square to each end of the remaining four units from step 3. Press the seams toward the squares.

8. Sew a unit from step 7 to the right side of a unit from step 6 as shown. Once again, be sure the gold triangles are next to the pieced squares. Press the seam toward the unit from step 7.

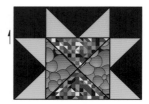

9. Arrange the four 6½" black squares, the four units from step 8, and the center unit from step 2 as shown to make the block. Sew the units together into rows. Press the seams of the top and bottom rows toward the black squares. Press the middle-row seams toward the center square. Sew the rows together to make the block. Press the seams toward the top and bottom rows.

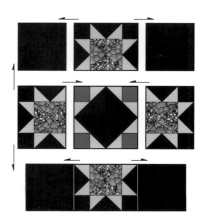

Quilt Assembly

1. Refer to "Borders with Straight-Cut Corners" on page 85 before adding the borders to your quilt. Sew a 1" x 20½" orange tone-on-tone strip to each side of the quilt top and press the seams toward the borders. Sew the 1" x 21½" orange tone-on-tone strips to the top and bottom of the quilt top and press the seams toward the border strip.

2. Sew a 3½" x 21½" autumn floral strip to each side of the quilt top and press the seams toward the borders. Sew the 3½" x 27½" autumn floral strips to the top and bottom of the quilt top and press the seams toward the borders.

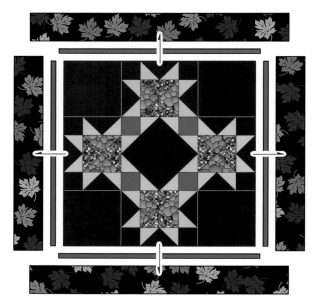

Quilt Assembly Diagram

Finishing

1. If you plan to have your quilt professionally machine quilted, refer to "Professional Quilting" on page 88 before continuing this section.

2. Cut the backing fabric into a 32" x 32" square.

3. Mark the quilt top if necessary. Layer the top with the batting and backing and baste the layers together using your preferred method (refer to "Preparing to Quilt" on page 87).

4. Hand or machine quilt as desired (refer to "Quilting Techniques" on page 87). This quilt was professionally machine quilted. Feathered wreaths were quilted with contrasting gold thread in the five black squares, and gold thread was also used to make large flower designs in the four star points of the wreath. Black thread was used to quilt the vine-and-leaf design that fills the border.

5. Remove any basting and trim the excess batting and backing fabric even with the edges of the quilt top. Join the three 2½"-wide black strips end to end with diagonal seams and bind the quilt (refer to "Binding" on page 89).

6. Make a label for your quilt that includes your name, the city and state where you live, the date, and any other interesting information, and stitch it to the back of your quilt.

Autumn Welcome

For a softer feel, use autumn fabrics in lighter shades of beige, brown, and purple. Laura wanted me to have a choice, so she made two wreath quilts that look quite different. This one belongs to her husband, John, because he liked it best. Make one of your own and hang it in your foyer to greet your guests.

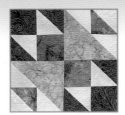

Lightning Bug Lagoon

My dear friend Laura offered to make a quilt for my book. She loves batik fabrics, so we chose batiks in beautiful evening shades for the Fireflies blocks. I remember catching fireflies on warm summer evenings and watching them glow until it was time to set them free and go to bed. This quilt is a gift for Laura's sweet daughter Bria. Enjoy!

Materials

Yardages are based on 42"-wide fabric.

1⅝ yards of batik print for outer border

1¼ yards of pink batik for blocks

1 yard of dark blue batik for inner border and binding

1 yard of purple batik for blocks

⅞ yard of light blue batik for blocks

⅞ yard of medium blue batik for blocks

5 yards of fabric for backing

67" x 83" piece of batting

Cutting

All cutting dimensions include ¼" seam allowances. Instructions are for cutting strips across the fabric width.

From the pink batik, cut:
8 strips, 4⅞" x 42"; crosscut into 60 squares, 4⅞" x 4⅞". Cut 24 squares once diagonally to yield 48 triangles.

From the purple batik, cut:
3 strips, 4½" x 42"; crosscut into 24 squares, 4½" x 4½"
3 strips, 4⅞" x 42"; crosscut into 24 squares, 4⅞" x 4⅞"

From the medium blue batik, cut:
3 strips, 4½" x 42"; crosscut into 24 squares, 4½" x 4½"
2 strips, 4⅞" x 42"; crosscut into 12 squares, 4⅞" x 4⅞"

From the light blue batik, cut:
3 strips, 8⅞" x 42"; crosscut into 12 squares, 8⅞" x 8⅞". Cut each square once diagonally to yield 24 triangles.

From the dark blue batik, cut:
6 strips, 1½" x 42"
8 binding strips, 2½" x 42"

From the batik print, cut:
8 strips, 6½" x 42"

Designed by Laurie Bevan. Pieced by Laura Roberts, Lafayette, Colorado.
Quilted by Janet Fogg, Lake Oswego, Oregon.

Quilt Size: 62½" x 78½" • **Block Size:** 16" • **Block Name:** Fireflies

Block Assembly

1. Draw a diagonal line on the wrong side of 36 pink 4⅞" squares.

2. With right sides together, place a marked pink square on each purple and medium blue 4⅞" square. Sew ¼" from each side of the drawn line. Cut the squares apart on the line and press the seams toward the purple and medium blue triangles.

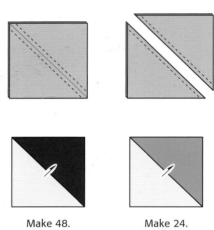

Make 48.   Make 24.

3. Sew a pink triangle to each side of the medium blue triangle in the triangle squares from step 2 as shown. Press the seams toward the pink triangles.

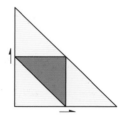

4. Sew a light blue triangle to each triangle unit from step 3 as shown. Press the seams toward the light blue triangles. These units should measure 8½" x 8½".

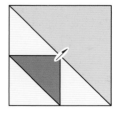

Make 24.

5. Sew a 4½" medium blue square to 24 of the purple triangle squares from step 2 as shown. Press the seams toward the medium blue squares. Sew a purple 4½" square to the remaining 24 purple triangle squares as shown. Press the seams toward the purple squares. Sew these two units together to make 8½" x 8½" four-patch units. Press the seams toward the purple squares. Pay careful attention to the diagram to place the colors correctly.

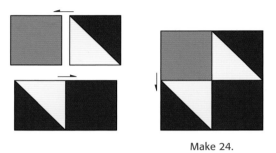

Make 24.

6. Sew a step 4 unit to each step 5 unit. Press the seams toward the step 4 units.

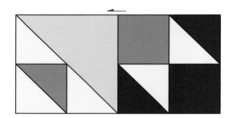

7. Sew two step 6 units together as shown to make each block. Once again, pay attention to the block diagram for correct color placement and pressing directions.

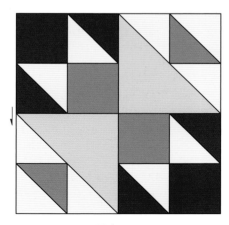

Make 12.

Quilt Assembly

1. Lay out the blocks into four horizontal rows of three blocks each as shown. If you rotate every other block 180º, the center seams in the blocks will be opposing. Sew each row together and press the seams in opposite directions from row to row. Sew the rows together and press the seams in one direction.

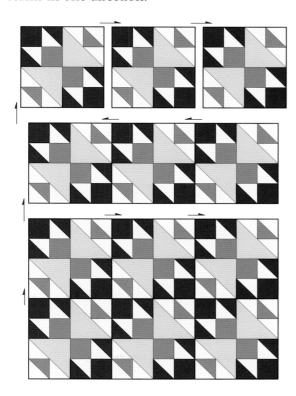

2. Refer to "Borders with Straight-Cut Corners" on page 85 before adding the borders to your quilt. Sew three of the 1½"-wide dark blue strips together end to end. Repeat with the remaining three 1½"-wide strips. From *each* long strip, cut a 64½"-long side border and a 50½"-long top/bottom border.

3. Sew a side border to each side of the quilt top and press the seams toward the borders. Sew the top and bottom borders to the quilt top and press the seams toward the borders.

4. Sew two of the 6½"-wide batik-print strips together end to end. Repeat to make a total of four long strips. From *each of two* of the long strips, cut a 66½"-long side border. Trim each of the remaining two long strips to 62½" for the top/bottom borders.

5. Sew a side border to each side of the quilt top and press the seams toward the borders. Sew the top and bottom borders to the quilt top and press the seams toward the borders.

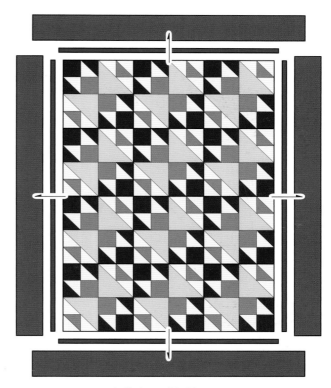

Quilt Assembly Diagram

Finishing

1. If you plan to have your quilt professionally machine quilted, refer to "Professional Quilting" on page 88 before continuing this section.

2. Cut the backing fabric into two equal lengths, remove the selvages, and sew the two pieces together along the length to make a backing with a vertical seam. Press the seam to one side. Your backing should be at least 67" wide and 83" long.

3. Mark the quilt top if necessary. Layer the top with the batting and backing and baste the layers together using your preferred method (refer to "Preparing to Quilt" on page 87).

4. Hand or machine quilt as desired (refer to "Quilting Techniques" on page 87). This quilt was professionally machine quilted. It was completely covered with ferns, flowers, and vines, and the background was quilted with a network of curves and swirls.

5. Remove any basting and trim the excess batting and backing fabric even with the edges of the quilt top. Join the eight 2½"-wide dark blue strips end to end with diagonal seams and bind the quilt (refer to "Binding" on page 89).

6. Make a label for your quilt that includes your name, the city and state where you live, the date, and any other interesting information, and stitch it to the back of your quilt.

Monochromatic Fireflies

This block is made from some of my favorite orange fabrics. The small beige-print triangles represent the "fireflies" and should be a light value. Play with different medium- and dark-value fabrics for the other pieces in the block.

Whispering Windmills

I've always wanted to make a quilt with all neutral-colored fabrics. When I found this beautiful beige floral, I knew I could make it work. Subtle value differences between the fabrics let the windmills stand out in the blocks. It's fun to try something different!

Materials

Yardages are based on 42"-wide fabric.

3 yards of beige floral for blocks, outer border, and binding

1 yard of beige tone-on-tone for blocks

1 yard of white-on-beige print for blocks

1 yard of light taupe tone-on-tone for blocks

⅜ yard of taupe print for inner border

5 yards of fabric for backing

66" x 82" piece of batting

Cutting

All cutting dimensions include ¼" seam allowances. Instructions are for cutting strips across the fabric width unless otherwise specified.

From the beige floral, cut:
3 strips, 10" x 42"; crosscut into 12 squares, 10" x 10"

From the *lengthwise* grain of the remaining beige floral, cut:
4 strips, 6½" wide
4 binding strips, 2½" wide

From the beige tone-on-tone print, cut:
3 strips, 10" x 42"; crosscut into 12 squares, 10" x 10"

From the white-on-beige print, cut:
3 strips, 10" x 42"; crosscut into 12 squares, 10" x 10"

From the light taupe tone-on-tone, cut:
3 strips, 10" x 42"; crosscut into 12 squares, 10" x 10"

From the taupe print, cut:
6 strips, 1¼" x 42"

Block Assembly

1. Place a 10" beige floral square on top of a 10" beige tone-on-tone square, right sides together. Draw two diagonal lines on the wrong side of the beige floral square as shown. Beginning at one corner, sew ¼" to the right of the line you're following until you reach the intersecting line. With your needle down on this line, turn the squares 90° and sew on the other diagonal line for ½". With your needle down, turn the squares back 90° and continue sewing, now with your stitching ¼" to the left of the first line, until you reach the opposite corner. Remove the squares from your machine and

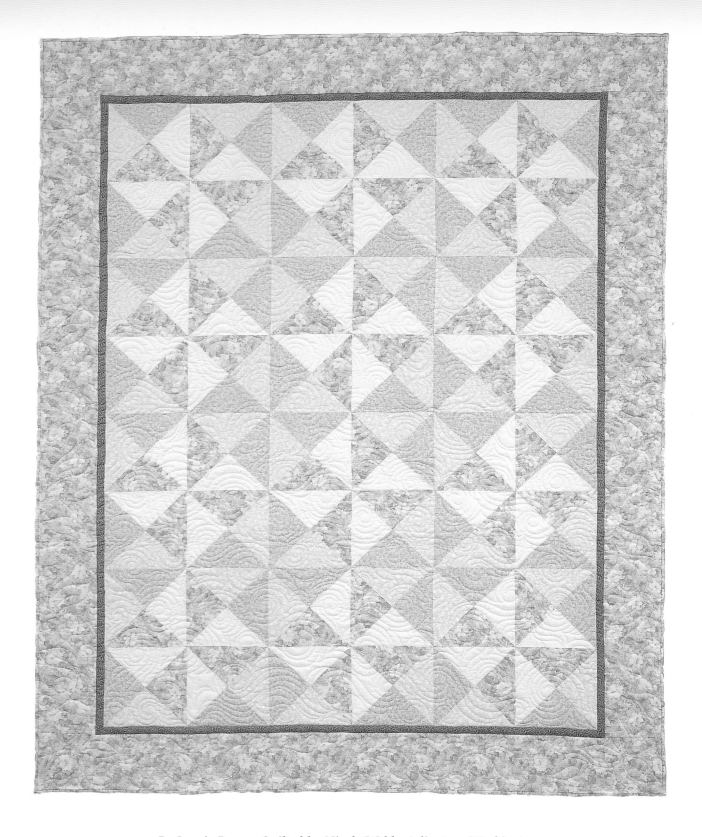

By Laurie Bevan. Quilted by Nicole Webb, Arlington, Washington.

Quilt Size: 62" x 78" • **Block Size:** 16" • **Block Name:** Electric Fan

sew the other diagonal line in the same manner. Cut along both diagonal lines and press each seam toward the floral fabric. Repeat this step with the remaining beige floral and beige tone-on-tone squares.

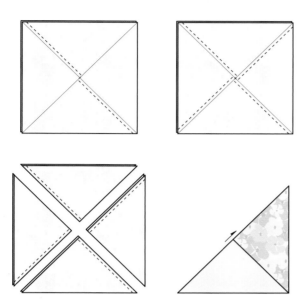

2. Repeat step 1 with the light taupe tone-on-tone squares on top of the white-on-beige squares. Press the seams toward the light taupe fabric.

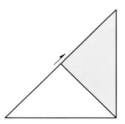

3. Sew each pieced triangle from step 1 to a pieced triangle from step 2 as shown. Press the seams toward the floral fabric. Trim these squares to 8½" x 8½". Be sure to center your squares so you don't cut off any points.

Make 48.

4. Sew four of the squares from step 3 together as shown to make each block. Be sure the floral fabric is in the correct position to make the windmill.

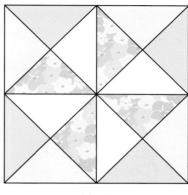

Make 12.

Quilt Assembly

1. Lay out the blocks into four horizontal rows of three blocks each. Sew the blocks together into rows and press the seams in opposite directions from row to row. Sew the rows together and press the seams in one direction.

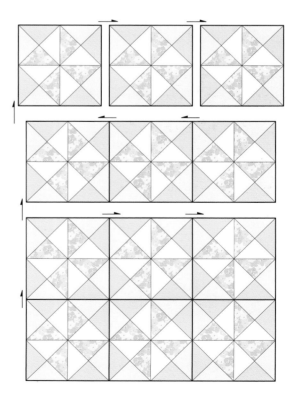

2. Refer to "Borders with Straight-Cut Corners" on page 85 before adding the borders to your quilt. Sew three of the 1¼"-wide taupe print strips together end to end. Repeat with the remaining three taupe print strips. From *each* long strip, cut one 64½"-long side border strip and one 50"-long top/bottom border strip.

3. Sew a side border to each side of the quilt top and press the seams toward the borders. Sew the top and bottom borders to the quilt top and press the seams toward the borders.

4. Trim two of the 6½"-wide beige floral strips to 66" long. Sew these borders to each side of the quilt top and press the seams toward the borders. Trim the remaining two 6½"-wide beige floral strips to 62" long. Sew these borders to the top and bottom of the quilt top and press the seams toward the borders.

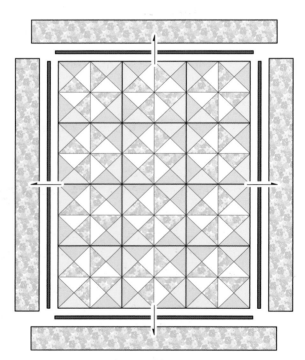

Quilt Assembly Diagram

Finishing

1. If you plan to have your quilt professionally machine quilted, refer to "Professional Quilting" on page 88 before continuing this section.

2. Cut the backing fabric into two equal lengths, remove the selvages, and sew the two pieces together along the length to make a backing with a vertical seam. Press the seam to one side. Your backing should be at least 66" wide and 82" long.

3. Mark the quilt top if necessary. Layer the top with the batting and backing and baste the layers together using your preferred method (refer to "Preparing to Quilt" on page 87).

4. Hand or machine quilt as desired (refer to "Quilting Techniques" on page 87). This quilt was professionally machine quilted. The center was filled with swirling curves that represent the wind, the inner border was outline quilted, and the floral border was quilted with a vine with leaves and curlicues.

5. Remove any basting and trim the excess batting and backing fabric even with the edges of the quilt top. Join the four 2½"-wide beige floral strips end to end with diagonal seams and bind the quilt (refer to "Binding" on page 89).

6. Make a label for your quilt that includes your name, the city and state where you live, the date, and any other interesting information, and stitch it to the back of your quilt.

Spring Breeze

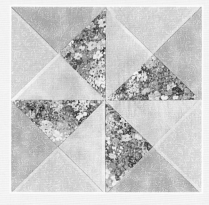

A pretty floral fabric and three colors that coordinate with it make a great springtime variation for the Electric Fan block.

For All My Sisters

Sister's Choice is another one of my favorite blocks. It makes me think of my sister, Robin, and of all my good friends who love me like a sister. Quilting is a hobby that gives us a feeling of "sisterhood" with all the women who share our passion for patchwork—those we know now, and those from the past and in the future.

Materials

Yardages are based on 42"-wide fabric.

4 yards of beige floral for alternate squares, side and corner triangles, and border

1⅝ yards of small-scale beige print for blocks

1⅜ yards of red floral for blocks

⅝ yard of green print for blocks

1 yard of green stripe for binding

5½ yards of fabric for backing

75" x 96" piece of batting

Cutting

All cutting dimensions include ¼" seam allowances. Instructions are for cutting strips across the fabric width.

From the small-scale beige print, cut:
5 strips, 3⅞" x 42"; crosscut into 48 squares, 3⅞" x 3⅞"
9 strips, 3½" x 42"; crosscut into 96 squares, 3½" x 3½"

From the red floral, cut:
5 strips, 3⅞" x 42"; crosscut into 48 squares, 3⅞" x 3⅞"
6 strips, 3½" x 42"; crosscut into 60 squares, 3½" x 3½"

From the green print, cut:
5 strips, 3½" x 42"; crosscut into 48 squares, 3½" x 3½"

From the beige floral, cut:
Note: To get the most out of your fabric, follow these cutting instructions exactly.

3 strips, 22½" x 42"; crosscut *each* strip into:
- 1 square (3 total), 22½" x 22½"; cut the square twice diagonally to yield 4 side triangles (12 total). You will use 10 and have 2 left over.
- 1 square (3 total), 15½" x 15½"
2 strips, 15½" x 42"; crosscut into:
- 3 squares, 15½" x 15½"
- 2 squares, 11½" x 11½"; cut each square once diagonally to yield 4 corner triangles
8 strips, 3½" x 42"

By Laurie Bevan. Quilted by Pam Clarke, Spokane, Washington.

Quilt Size: 70¼" x 91½" • **Block Size:** 15" • **Block Name:** Sister's Choice

Block Assembly

1. Draw a diagonal line on the wrong side of each 3⅞" beige square. Place each square right sides together with a 3⅞" red square. Sew ¼" from each side of the drawn line. Cut the squares apart on the line and press the seams toward the red triangles.

Make 96.

2. To make each block, arrange eight triangle squares from step 1, five 3½" red squares, eight 3½" beige squares, and four 3½" green squares as shown. Stitch the pieces in each row together. Press the seams in the directions indicated. Sew the rows together. Pressing suggestions are given, but you may press these seams in either direction.

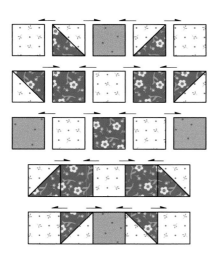

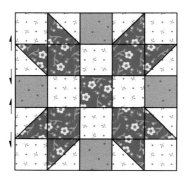

Make 12.

Quilt Assembly

1. Lay out the pieced blocks, the 15½"-square beige floral blocks, and the side and corner triangles in diagonal rows as shown.

2. Sew the blocks and side triangles in each row together and press the seams toward the alternate blocks and triangles. Sew the rows together and press the seams in either direction. Sew a corner triangle to each corner of the quilt top and press the seams toward the corners.

3. Refer to "Arranging On-Point Layouts" on page 84 to trim the edges of the quilt top, leaving a ¼" seam allowance beyond the block points. Square up the four corners.

4. Refer to "Borders with Straight-Cut Corners" on page 85 before adding the borders to your quilt. Sew four of the 3½"-wide beige floral strips together end to end. Repeat with the remaining four strips to make two long strips. From *each* of these long strips, cut one side border 85½" long and one top/bottom border 70¼" long.

5. Sew a side border to each side of the quilt top and press the seams toward the borders. Sew a top/bottom border to the top and bottom of the quilt top and press the seams toward the borders.

Quilt Assembly Diagram

Finishing

1. If you plan to have your quilt professionally machine quilted, refer to "Professional Quilting" on page 88 before continuing this section.

2. Cut the backing fabric into two equal lengths, remove the selvages, and sew the two pieces together along the length to make a backing with a vertical seam. Press the seam to one side. Your backing should be at least 75" wide and 96" long.

3. Mark the quilt top if necessary. Layer the top with the batting and backing and baste the layers together using your preferred method (refer to "Preparing to Quilt" on page 87).

4. Hand or machine quilt as desired (refer to "Quilting Techniques" on page 87). This quilt was professionally machine quilted. The blocks were quilted with a diagonal grid and the alternate squares were filled with feathers. The side and corner triangles were quilted with feathered hearts and the border with an interlocking heart design.

5. Remove any basting and trim the excess batting and backing fabric even with the edges of the quilt top. From the green striped fabric, cut enough 2½"-wide bias strips to equal at least 340" when the strips are joined (refer to "Cutting Bias Binding" on page 89). Bind the quilt (refer to "Attaching the Binding" on page 90).

6. Make a label for your quilt that includes your name, the city and state where you live, the date, and any other interesting information, and stitch it to the back of your quilt.

Sisters in Summer

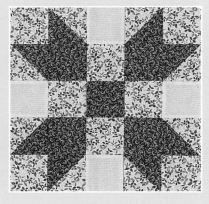

When you need only three colors to make a quilt block, there is no palette more cheerful than blue, yellow, and white (with a hint of green, as in this block.) Make this quilt variation for one of your "sisters." I'm sure she'll love it!

Graphic Design

The black-and-white floral fabric used in this quilt is a memory from my past. As a teenager in the early 1970s, I used to buy black-and-white posters, very much like this fabric, that came with a set of felt-tipped pens to color the designs on the poster. Coloring the white spaces was so much fun, and a group of friends could work on one poster together. Someday, I'm going to buy a set of fabric markers and start coloring these flowers.

Materials

Yardages are based on 42"-wide fabrics.

2¼ yards of black-and-white floral for blocks and outer border

1⅜ yards of black-with-white hearts print for blocks

1⅜ yards of white-with-black stars print for blocks

1 yard of black solid for inner border and binding

⅝ yard of black-with-white flowers print for blocks

⅝ yard of white-with-black swirls print for blocks

5 yards of fabric for backing

72" x 88" piece of batting

Cutting

All cutting dimensions include ¼" seam allowances. Instructions are for cutting strips across the fabric width unless otherwise specified.

From the black-and-white floral, cut:
2 strips, 4½" x 42"; crosscut into 12 squares, 4½" x 4½"

From the *lengthwise* grain of the remaining black-and-white floral, cut:
4 strips, 9½" wide

From the white-with-black swirls print, cut:
2 strips, 3¾" x 42"; crosscut into 12 squares, 3¾" x 3¾". Cut each square once diagonally to yield 24 triangles.
2 strips, 4⅞" x 42"; crosscut into 12 squares, 4⅞" x 4⅞". Cut each square once diagonally to yield 24 triangles.

From the black-with-white flowers print, cut:
2 strips, 3¾" x 42"; crosscut into 12 squares, 3¾" x 3¾". Cut each square once diagonally to yield 24 triangles.
2 strips, 4⅞" x 42"; crosscut into 12 squares, 4⅞" x 4⅞". Cut each square once diagonally to yield 24 triangles.

By Laurie Bevan. Quilted by Janet Fogg, Lake Oswego, Oregon.

Quilt Size: 68" x 84" • **Block Size:** 16" • **Block Name:** Square on Square

From the white-with-black stars print, cut:

2 strips, 6½" x 42"; crosscut into 12 squares, 6½" x 6½". Cut each square once diagonally to yield 24 triangles.

3 strips, 8⅞" x 42"; crosscut into 12 squares, 8⅞" x 8⅞". Cut each square once diagonally to yield 24 triangles.

From the black-with-white hearts print, cut:

2 strips, 6½" x 42"; crosscut into 12 squares, 6½" x 6½". Cut each square once diagonally to yield 24 triangles.

3 strips, 8⅞" x 42"; crosscut into 12 squares, 8⅞" x 8⅞". Cut each square once diagonally to yield 24 triangles.

From the black solid, cut:

6 strips, 1¼" x 42"

8 binding strips, 2½" x 42"

Block Assembly

The long edge of every triangle is cut on the bias. The side of the square you're sewing it to is not, so always sew with the triangle on the bottom to avoid any stretching. Positioning the pieces this way will also help you hit the point of the square perfectly every time.

Positive Blocks

1. For each block, fold a black-and-white floral square in half top to bottom and lightly crease the fold. Fold two of the 3¾" white-with-black swirls triangles in half along the long edge and lightly crease the fold. Match the folds of the triangle with those of the floral square and sew one triangle to each side. Press the seams toward the triangles.

2. Fold the floral square in half side to side and lightly crease the fold. Fold two more of the 3¾" white-with-black swirls triangles in half

along the long edge and lightly crease the folds. Match the folds of these triangles with those on the floral square and sew one triangle to the top and one to the bottom. Press the seams toward the triangles. Trim this square to 6⅛" x 6⅛", centering the floral square and leaving ¼" beyond each of the square points.

3. The next round of triangles that will be added is the 4⅞" black-with-white flowers. You no longer need to fold the floral square because you will be matching the fold of each new triangle with the point at the center of each side of the square from the previous step. Fold, sew, and press these four triangles as in steps 1 and 2. Trim this square to 8½" x 8½".

4. Add the 6½" white-with-black stars triangles to the square as in steps 1 and 2. Trim this square to 11¾" x 11¾".

5. Add the 8⅞" black-with-white hearts triangles to the square as in steps 1 and 2. Trim this square to 16½" x 16½".

Positive Block
Make 6.

Negative Blocks

1. For each block, fold a black-and-white floral square in half top to bottom and lightly crease the fold. Fold two of the 3¾" black-with-white flowers triangles in half along the long edge and crease the fold. Match the folds of the triangle with those of the floral square and sew one triangle to each side. Press the seams toward the triangles.

2. Fold the floral square in half side to side and lightly crease the fold. Fold two more of the 3¾" black-with-white flowers triangles in half along the long edge and lightly crease the folds. Match the folds of these triangles with those on the floral square and sew one triangle to the top and one to the bottom. Press the seams toward the triangles. Trim

this square to 6⅛" x 6⅛", centering the floral square and leaving ¼" beyond each of the square points.

3. The next round of triangles that will be added is the 4⅞" white-with-black swirls. You no longer need to fold the floral square because you will be matching the fold of each new triangle with the point at the center of each side of the square from the previous step. Fold, sew, and press these four triangles as in steps 1 and 2. Trim this square to 8½" x 8½".

4. Add the 6½" black-with-white hearts triangles to the square as in steps 1 and 2. Trim this square to 11¾" x 11¾".

5. Add the 8⅞" white-with-black stars triangles to the square as in steps 1 and 2. Trim this square to 16½" x 16½".

Negative Block
Make 6.

Quilt Assembly

1. Lay out the blocks in four horizontal rows of three blocks each as shown, alternating the negative and positive blocks within each row and from row to row. Sew the blocks into rows and press the seams toward the positive blocks. Sew the rows together and press the seams in one direction.

2. Refer to "Borders with Straight-Cut Corners" on page 85 before adding the borders to your quilt. Sew three of the 1¼"-wide black solid strips together end to end. Repeat with the remaining three strips. From *each* of these long strips, cut one side border 64½" long and one top/bottom border 50" long.

3. Sew a side border strip to each side of the quilt top and press the seams toward the borders. Sew the top/bottom border strips to the top and bottom of the quilt top and press the seams toward the borders.

4. Trim two of the 9½"-wide floral strips to 66" long. Sew these border strips to each side of the quilt top and press the seams toward the borders. Trim the remaining two floral strips to 68" long. Sew these border strips to the top and bottom of the quilt top and press the seams toward the borders.

Quilt Assembly Diagram

Finishing

1. If you plan to have your quilt professionally machine quilted, refer to "Professional Quilting" on page 88 before continuing this section.

2. Cut the backing fabric into two equal lengths, remove the selvages, and sew the two pieces together along the length to make a backing with a vertical seam. Press the seam to one side. Your backing should be at least 72" wide and 88" long.

3. Mark the quilt top if necessary. Layer the top with the batting and backing and baste the layers together using your preferred method (refer to "Preparing to Quilt" on page 87).

4. Hand or machine quilt as desired (refer to "Quilting Techniques" on page 87). This quilt was professionally machine quilted all over with a combination of large flowers like those in the border print and medium-sized meandering.

5. Remove any basting and trim the excess batting and backing fabric even with the edges of the quilt top. Join the eight 2½"-wide black solid strips end to end with diagonal seams and bind the quilt (refer to "Binding" on page 89).

6. Make a label for your quilt that includes your name, the city and state where you live, the date, and any other interesting information, and stitch it to the back of your quilt.

Rainbows

What a contrast—from no color to all colors! These bright fabrics would make a perfect quilt for a little girl. I have reversed the color scheme in the two blocks to make one "positive" and one "negative." Maybe I'll finish this one and give it to someone special.

Quiltmaking Basics

The project instructions provided in this book assume that you already have a basic knowledge of how to make a quilt. The techniques I used for making these quilts are offered on the next few pages. Please refer to this information at any time during the quiltmaking process to learn about a step you are unfamiliar with or to review a technique you already know how to do. I hope you find this information helpful so you will truly enjoy the "process" of quiltmaking.

Fabrics

I use only 100%-cotton fabrics of the highest quality I can afford for my quilts. I always wash my fabrics as soon as I get them home to remove any chemicals on the fabric and to be sure the dyes won't run. Diagonally cut a little piece off each of the four corners of a fabric before you put it in the washing machine; this helps prevent excessive fraying. Remove the fabrics promptly from the dryer and simply shake them out and fold them. If you're not going to use them right away, why bother to iron them? You'll just have to do it again later. If you keep your fabrics sorted by color, collection, theme, project, or some other criteria, it is easier to find a particular one you're looking for when it's time to use it in a quilt. Fabric is the paint for our canvas, and you can never have too many colors!

Supplies

Rotary-cutting tools: A cutting mat, a rotary cutter, and a long acrylic ruler are the minimum tools required to cut the strips and pieces for the projects in this book. A mat that measures 24" x 36" is great, but one that is 18" x 24" will work fine. Any rotary cutter will do, but a sharp blade is a must. Always keep an extra new blade with your supplies. A long ruler that is 6" x 24" will work for all

the projects. A 6" or 8" square ruler is nice to have as well for crosscutting strips into squares and rectangles. For big-block quilts, you might want to invest in a 20½"-square ruler for squaring up your finished blocks.

Sewing machine: A machine in good working order is essential to piece the quilt tops in this book. A straight stitch with even tension and an accurate ¼" seam guide are all you need. If you want to machine quilt your own tops, you will need a walking-foot or darning-foot attachment. Some sewing machine models have a built-in walking foot.

Iron and pressing surface: Any iron that has a cotton temperature setting and a steam option will work for quiltmaking. A firm, flat surface with insulation and a cloth cover, such as an ironing board or pressing pad, are needed as well. A small surface is fine for pressing blocks, but a larger area is desirable for pressing entire rows and yardage before cutting.

Thread: Use good-quality, 100%-cotton thread for piecing your quilt tops. White, beige, gray, and black are four colors to definitely have on hand. With these four colors, you can piece just about anything. Sometimes, when hand turning a binding, I may need a special color to match the fabric, and then I use a cotton-covered polyester thread, simply because there are more color choices.

Needles: Use a size 70/10 or 80/12 sewing-machine needle for piecing your quilt tops. Change your needle after each major project for best stitch results. A size 90/14 needle is used for machine quilting. Short, sharp hand-sewing needles called Betweens are designed for hand quilting. A standard hand-sewing needle is used for stitching the binding to the backing.

Pins: I prefer long, fine pins with heads for my piecing. The finer the pin, the flatter your layers will lie. Pins with heads are easier to remove, easier to see when your needle reaches them, and certainly faster to find on the floor.

Scissors: A must for your basic supplies is a good, sharp pair of large scissors used only for cutting fabric. A small pair of scissors next to your sewing machine is great for snipping threads.

Seam ripper: This is an extremely valuable tool that is used to remove stitches from incorrectly sewn seams. I own several.

Template plastic: This clear or frosted plastic comes in sheets (available at quilt shops) and is used to make durable, accurate templates.

Marking tools: You will want to have a sharp lead pencil, a white chalk pencil, and a very fine black fabric marker on hand for drawing lines on the wrong side of fabrics for some of the piecing techniques in this book. Lead pencils, chalk pencils, or special pens can be used for marking quilting designs. Before marking your top, test the tool on your fabric to be sure you can remove the marks easily.

Rotary Cutting

All of the strips and pieces for the projects in this book were rotary cut. If you have never used a rotary cutter for making quilts, please read through these basic directions. For a more thorough lesson, see *Shortcuts: A Concise Guide to Rotary Cutting* by Donna Lynn Thomas (Martingale & Company, 1999.) Remember: Always measure twice and cut once!

Cutting Crosswise Strips

1. Fold your fabric in half along the lengthwise grain, matching selvages as best as possible. With the fold closest to you, place your fabric along the bottom horizontal line of your cutting mat. Be sure your fabric lies flat. Use your long ruler and align one of the vertical lines on the ruler with a vertical line on your mat so that the ruler completely covers both cut ends of the fabric. Cut along the right side of the ruler and discard the uneven scrap.

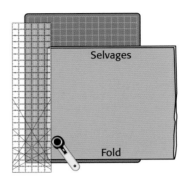

2. To cut the strips, align the correct vertical measurement line on your ruler with the previously cut edge of the fabric. Cut the strip along the right side of the ruler. Continue cutting as many fabric strips as are required for the project. (Reverse the procedure in steps 1 and 2 if you are a left-handed quilter.)

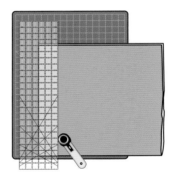

Cutting Lengthwise Strips

1. Fold the piece of fabric in half along the crosswise grain, matching the selvage edges. Because of the length of your piece, you will need to fold the fabric in half again along the crosswise grain; be sure to match the selvage edges. With the double fold closest to you, place your fabric along the bottom horizontal line of your cutting mat. Be sure your fabric

lies flat. Use your long ruler and align one of the vertical lines on the ruler with a vertical line on your mat so that the ruler completely covers the left selvage edge of the fabric. Cut along the right side of the ruler and discard the selvage.

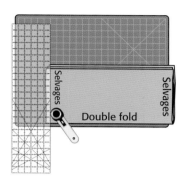

2. To cut the strips, align the correct vertical measurement line on your ruler with the previously cut edge of the fabric. Cut the strip along the right side of the ruler. Continue cutting as many fabric strips as are required for the project. (Reverse the procedure in steps 1 and 2 if you are a left-handed quilter.)

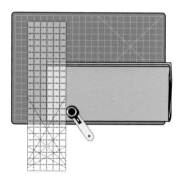

Cutting Squares

Lay the strips that have been cut to the required width on your cutting mat. You may stack strips up to six layers thick to cut many squares of the same size. Use your ruler as in step 1 of "Cutting Lengthwise Strips" on page 80 to trim the selvage ends from the strips. Align the left edge of the

strips with the correct ruler marking. The length you cut will be the same as the width of the strip. Cut as many squares as you need. (You will align the right edge of the strips with the correct ruler markings if you are a left-handed quilter.)

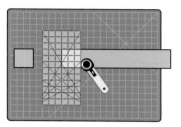

Cutting Rectangles

Lay the strips that have been cut to the required width on your cutting mat. You may stack strips up to six layers thick to cut many rectangles of the same size. Use your ruler as in step 1 of "Cutting Lengthwise Strips" on page 80 to trim the selvage ends from the strips. Align the left edge of the strips with the correct ruler marking. The length you cut will be the measurement of the rectangle (length or width) that is not the width of the strip. For example, if the strip width is 2½", then the length you cut will be 4½" to make a 2½" x 4½" rectangle. If the strip width is 4½", then the length you cut will be 2½".

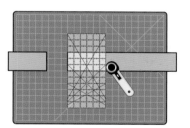

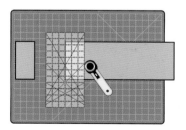

Cutting Squares Once Diagonally

Align the right edge of your ruler diagonally from corner to corner on each square and cut. You may stack squares up to six layers thick to diagonally cut many squares at once. (You will align the left edge of your ruler diagonally from corner to corner on each square and cut if you are a left-handed quilter.)

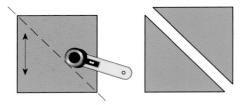

Cutting Squares Twice Diagonally

Make the first diagonal cut as above. Do not disturb the pieces and align the right edge of your ruler diagonally from one remaining uncut corner to the other uncut corner. Make the second cut. (You will align the left edge of your ruler diagonally from uncut corner to uncut corner if you are a left-handed quilter.)

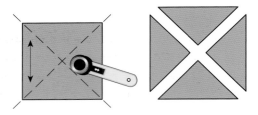

Machine Piecing

A stitched seam with even tension and an accurate ¼"-wide seam allowance are two of the most important requirements for quality machine piecing. Follow the instructions in your sewing-machine manual to properly adjust your thread tension. If your tension is too loose, your pieces may pull apart; if it's too tight, your seams will be puckered.

Some machines have a ¼" foot you can attach and then align your pieces with the edge of the foot as a guide. If you do not have this foot, you can measure ¼" away from your needle and use a piece of blue painter's tape or moleskin on your throat plate as a seam guide.

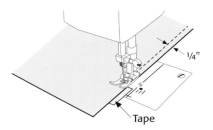

If your seam allowances are not exactly ¼", your blocks will be too large or too small. When you combine them with the other parts of the quilt top, such as alternate blocks or borders, the pieces will not fit together. As a seam-allowance test, sew three short 1½"-wide strips together as shown. If your seam allowances are accurate, the center strip will measure exactly 1" wide.

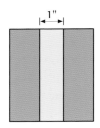

Chain Piecing

This time-saving technique allows you to save thread and piece many units at once.

1. Start with a small scrap of fabric and sew across it, stopping at the end of the fabric.

2. Feed the unit to be sewn under the presser foot until it almost butts up to the scrap. Sew the seam across this unit, stopping at the end.

3. Continue feeding all the units to be sewn through the machine without cutting between them.

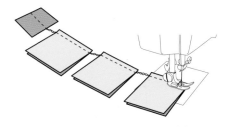

Chain Piecing

4. When all the units are sewn, remove the chain from the machine and clip the threads between the units.

Easing

When two pieces to be sewn together are different in size (no more than ⅛"), it is possible to make them fit together. Pin any intersections that should match and the raw edges; then pin in between to spread the excess fabric evenly. Sew the seam, placing the larger piece on the bottom. The feed dogs will ease the two pieces together.

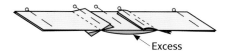

Excess

Pressing

To use steam or not to use steam, that is the question. Personally, I like to use just a hint of steam when piecing. I believe it makes the seams lie flatter, but it can also distort the shape of your piece. Be sure to *press* the seam, lifting the iron up and down, rather than using a back-and-forth ironing motion.

Press each piece on the wrong side first to "set" the seam. Then press the seam from the right side toward the fabric specified in the project instructions or in the direction of the pressing arrow on the illustration.

Most of the pressing instructions for the projects in this book are given so that when you sew two seamed units together, the seams will be pressed in opposite directions. This allows the seams to butt together and makes a perfectly matched intersection.

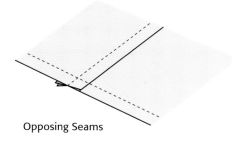

Opposing Seams

Assembling the Quilt Top

When all of your blocks are the same size and your borders are cut to the correct lengths, your completed quilt top will be a perfect square or rectangle and it will lie flat.

Squaring Up Blocks

All of your blocks need to be the same size in order to sew them together. Your blocks should measure the finished size given in the project plus ¼" on each side for seam allowances. For example, 15" finished blocks should measure 15½" before you sew them together.

Use a square ruler equal to or larger than the size of your blocks. For lickety-split blocks, that means you need a 20½"-square ruler. If you don't have one, I have given instructions in this section for using a long ruler as well.

If all your blocks are the same size, but not the exact size required for the project, you will need to adjust the measurements of the other parts of the quilt top, such as alternate blocks and borders, as necessary.

To square up blocks that are larger than required using a 20½"-square ruler: Center your ruler on the block and trim all four sides, but be sure to leave a ¼" seam allowance on each side past the points of the block design.

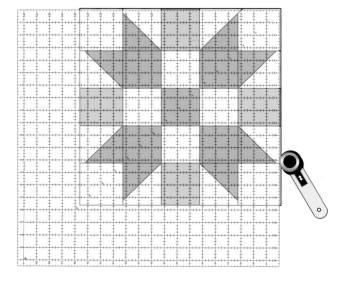

To square up blocks that are larger than required using a long ruler: Measure each side of your block using one edge of your long ruler. Calculate how much must be trimmed from each side. Align that measurement of your ruler with the left side of the block and trim. Be sure to leave a ¼" seam allowance past the points of the block design. Trim the remaining three sides and remeasure. Use one end of the long ruler (or a square ruler) to make sure each corner is square.

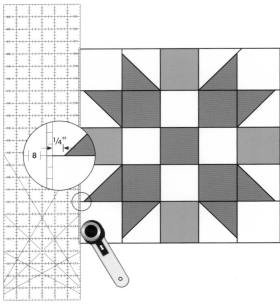

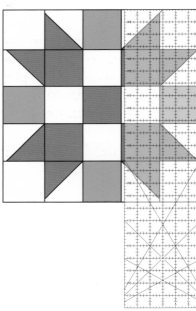

For any block that is too small: If the difference is ⅛" or less on each side, use the block as is and refer to "Easing" on page 83 to sew the small block to another block. If the difference is more than ⅛" on each side, check your seam allowances and resew where necessary.

Arranging Straight-Set Layouts

1. Lay out the blocks into the number of rows with the number of blocks in each row according to the quilt-assembly instructions and diagram. Pay careful attention to any special instructions about how to orient the blocks.

2. Sew the blocks together into horizontal rows and press the seam allowances in the direction given in the instructions or in the direction of the pressing arrows on the illustration. If no direction is given, press the seams of each row in the opposite direction.

3. Sew the rows together and be sure to match all the seam intersections. Press these seam allowances in the direction given in the project or to either side if no instructions are provided.

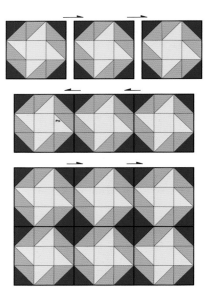

Arranging On-Point Layouts

1. Lay out the pieced blocks, alternate blocks, side triangles, and corner triangles according to the project diagram. A quilt top with 12 pieced blocks will have 6 alternate blocks, 10 side triangles, and 4 corner triangles.

2. Sew the pieced blocks, alternate blocks, and side triangles into diagonal rows. Press the seam allowances toward the alternate blocks and side triangles.

3. Sew the rows together, matching all the seam intersections. Press these seams in either direction.

4. Sew a corner triangle to each of the four corners. Press the seams toward the corners.

5. Use a long ruler to trim all four sides of the quilt top. Align the ¼" measurement line on the ruler with two points at the edge of the quilt top and trim, leaving exactly ¼" for seam allowances. Use the end of your long ruler or a square ruler to square up the four corners.

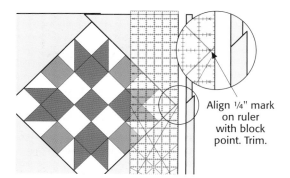

Align ¼" mark
on ruler
with block
point. Trim.

Borders with Straight-Cut Corners

1. Measure the length of the quilt top through the center. Cut two side border strips this length and the width indicated in the project cutting instructions. Mark the center of each border strip and each side of the quilt top. Pin the borders to the quilt top, matching centers and raw edges. Pin as necessary to make the two pieces ease together. Sew the border strips to the quilt top and press the seam allowances toward the borders.

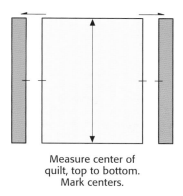

Measure center of
quilt, top to bottom.
Mark centers.

2. Measure the width of the quilt top through the center, including the side borders you just added. Cut a top and bottom border strip this length and the width indicated in the project cutting instructions. Mark the center of each border strip and the center of the top and bottom of the quilt top. Pin the borders to the quilt top, matching centers and raw edges. Pin as necessary to make the two pieces ease together. Sew the border strips to the quilt top and press the seam allowances toward the borders.

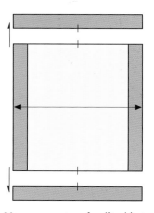

Measure center of quilt, side to
side, including border strips.
Mark centers.

Borders with Mitered Corners

1. Calculate the finished outside dimensions of your quilt top, including the borders. For example, if your top measures 48½" x 64½" and you want an 8"-wide finished border, your quilt top will then measure 64½" x 80½" after you attach the borders. Add approximately 4" more to each of these measurements to give yourself a little extra for safety's sake. So for this example, you would cut two side borders that are each 85" long and a top and bottom border that are each 69" long. (In this book, the length to cut your border strips is given in the project instructions.)

Note: If your quilt has more than one border, you can sew all the border strips together for each side first and then sew them all to the quilt top at once. When you are mitering the corners, be sure to match the seam intersections of each different border.

2. Mark the center of each of the border strips and the center of each of the four edges (sides, top, and bottom) of the quilt top with a pin. Use a pin to mark where each end of the quilt top will be on the border strips. Measure the length for the two side borders and the width for the top and bottom borders.

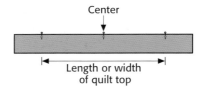

Center

Length or width
of quilt top

3. Pin one side border strip to the quilt top, matching center pins and aligning the end pins with the raw edges of the quilt top. Sew the seam, starting ¼" from the edge of the quilt top (backstitch at this point) and stopping ¼" from the other edge of the quilt top (backstitch at this point, too.) Press the seam toward the border. Repeat with the second side border and then add the top and bottom

borders in the same manner. Do not trim any of the excess fabric.

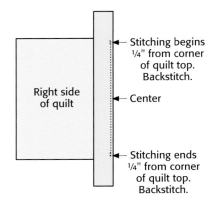

Right side
of quilt

Stitching begins
¼" from corner
of quilt top.
Backstitch.

Center

Stitching ends
¼" from corner
of quilt top.
Backstitch.

4. Lay out one corner of the quilt top on the ironing board, wrong side up. Fold each border back so that the two strips form a 45° angle at the corner. Use a ruler to make sure the corner is a perfect right angle, and then lightly press the folds.

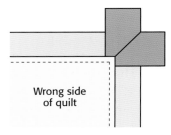

Wrong side
of quilt

5. Fold the quilt top so the right sides are together and the edges of the borders are aligned. Pin and sew the borders along the fold lines, starting at the previous stitching line (backstitch at this point) and sewing all the way to the outside edge. Press the seam open and check the right side of the corner to be sure the miter is good. Trim the excess fabric from the corner, leaving a ¼"-wide seam allowance.

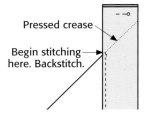

Pressed crease

Begin stitching
here. Backstitch.

6. Repeat steps 4 and 5 for each of the remaining corners.

Preparing to Quilt

You have several choices for quilting your project. You may quilt by hand or on your own sewing machine, or you may hire a professional machine quilter to quilt it for you. If you choose to use a professional machine quilter, refer to "Professional Quilting" on page 88 for preparation instructions. If you plan to quilt your project yourself, follow the instructions below.

Marking Your Quilt Top

Once again, you have several choices for marking your quilt top. Depending on the type of quilting you plan to do, you may not need to mark at all.

If you stitch in the ditch (along the seam lines), outline quilt a certain distance from the seam lines (usually ¼"), stipple quilt (small, random curving lines), or meander quilt (larger, random curving lines), you will not need to mark your quilt top.

You can use masking tape or blue painter's tape in any width to mark straight lines across your quilt top. This is especially useful for quilting diagonal grids. Tape small sections or one row at a time and remove the tape when you are through quilting that day, or the tape may leave a sticky residue on your quilt top.

If you wish to quilt a more intricate design using a template or quilting pattern, you will need to mark your quilt top so the design lines are visible enough to follow. See "Marking tools" on page 80 to choose the right marker for your project. Test the marker on scraps from your quilt top to be sure you can remove the marks easily. You will mark you quilt top before you layer it with batting and backing.

Layering and Basting Your Quilt

It is now time to make your quilt "sandwich." You will layer the backing, batting, and quilt top in preparation for quilting. Your backing should be at least 4" longer and wider than your quilt top. Follow the project instructions for piecing your backing if necessary. You may purchase batting in precut sizes or by the yard.

1. Lay out your backing, wrong side up, on a flat surface and tape or pin the edges to keep it taut. Be careful not to stretch it out of shape.

2. Center the batting on top of the backing and smooth out any wrinkles.

3. Center your pressed quilt top, right side up, on the batting. Be sure the edges of the top are parallel to the edges of the backing. Smooth out any wrinkles until the top is completely flat.

4. If you will be hand quilting, baste using a needle and thread. Start in the center of the quilt top and baste diagonally toward each corner. Next, baste a grid of horizontal and vertical lines 6" to 8" apart. Finally, baste around the edges.

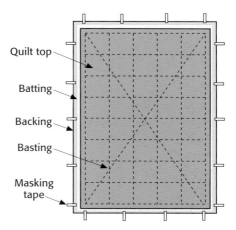

If you will be machine quilting, use large, rustproof safety pins. Place them about 6" to 8" away from the places where you plan to quilt.

Quilting Techniques

Most of the quilts in this book were machine quilted by talented professionals; one was hand quilted by a good friend. Only on rare occasions do I do my own quilting, but I have included instructions here so you will be able to do it yourself.

Hand Quilting

I have tried hand quilting only to learn it's not my cup of tea. If I want one of my quilts hand quilted, I find someone who enjoys that part of the quiltmaking process to do it for me.

Occasionally, I like to add some designs and color to one of my quilts with folk art–style hand quilting, which is done with a strand of pearl cotton and large stitches; that's all I can handle. For your benefit, the basics of hand quilting are explained below. For more information on hand quilting, refer to *Loving Stitches: A Guide to Fine Hand Quilting, Revised Edition,* by Jeana Kimball (Martingale & Company, 2003).

To quilt by hand, you will need short, sturdy needles (called Betweens), quilting thread, and a thimble to fit the middle finger of your sewing hand. Most quilters also use a frame or hoop to support their work. Use the smallest needle you can comfortably handle; the finer the needle, the smaller your stitches will be.

1. Thread your needle with a single strand of quilting thread about 18" long. Make a small knot and insert the needle in the top layer about 1" from the place where you want to start stitching. Pull the needle out at the point where quilting will begin and gently pull the thread until the knot pops through the top layer and into the batting.

2. Take small, evenly spaced stitches through all three quilt layers. Rock the needle up and down through all layers until you have three or four stitches on the needle. Place your other hand underneath the quilt so you can feel the needle point with the tip of your finger when a stitch is taken.

3. To end a line of quilting, make a small knot close to the last stitch; then backstitch, running the thread a needle's length through the batting. Gently pull the thread until the knot pops into the batting; clip the thread at the quilt's surface.

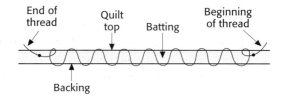

Machine Quilting

Machine quilting is great for all types of quilts, from wall hangings to bed-sized quilts. Refer to "Marking Your Quilt Top" and "Layering and Basting Your Quilt" on page 87 before you start to quilt your project.

For quilting straight lines, it is best to use a walking foot. This is a built-in feature on some sewing-machine models, but you can also buy a special foot to attach to your machine if you don't have one of those models. A walking foot feeds the top and bottom layers of fabric through the machine evenly so there is no puckering, bunching, or pulling.

For quilting almost any design other than straight lines, you will need a darning foot and the ability to drop or cover the feed dogs on your machine. When using a darning foot to quilt, you guide the fabric in the direction of the design rather than turning the fabric under the needle. Use this method for stipple or meander quilting, or to outline quilt a specific design.

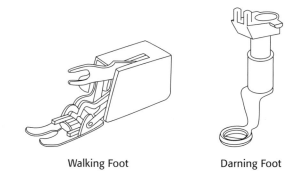

Walking Foot   Darning Foot

Professional Quilting

If you plan to have your quilt professionally machine quilted, ask your quilting friends to recommend a quilter they have used who does quality work. You can also ask at your local quilt shop for names of quilters in your area. If at all possible, ask to see samples of the quilter's work to be sure you will be satisfied with the quilting done on your quilt.

Contact the quilter and ask what preparations you need to do before bringing her your quilt. Usually you will not be layering the "sandwich" or basting and marking the top. Be sure to ask how much bigger the backing should be than the top and if she will be supplying the batting. Long-arm quilting machines use long rolls of batting that attach to the machine and roll out between your quilt top and backing fabric. Most professional quilters have a few types and weights to choose from. Professional machine quilting is a great option when you choose not to quilt your own project.

Adding a Hanging Sleeve

If you plan to hang your quilt on a wall for display, you will need to sew a sleeve on the back at the top of the quilt. You will put a rod or dowel inside the sleeve to evenly distribute the weight of the quilt when it hangs.

1. Use a piece of backing fabric (or muslin) cut 6" to 8" wide and 1" shorter than the width of your quilt. Fold the short ends under ½" and then another ½" to create a hem. Press the folds to keep the hem flat, and then sew ⅜" in from each edge.

2. Fold the fabric in half lengthwise, wrong sides together. Align the sleeve raw edges with the quilt back raw edge and machine baste across the top. When you sew the binding on, the sleeve will be firmly attached to the quilt.

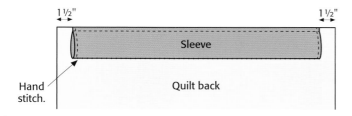

3. After the binding has been sewn on, blind-stitch the bottom of the sleeve to the quilt backing. Raise the bottom edge of the sleeve up a bit to provide a little room so the hanging rod does not put strain on the quilt.

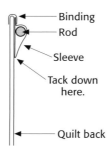

Binding

Even though I rarely do the quilting on my own quilts, I always add the binding to finish them off. I want to be the last person to work on them. After machine sewing the binding to the front, it is a pleasure to sit and hand stitch the binding to the back. I watch a favorite movie while I stitch and I'm done in no time.

Cutting Straight-Grain Binding

From your binding fabric, cut the number of strips required in the width given in the project instructions. If this information is not provided, cut strips 2¼" to 2¾" wide across the width of the fabric. I prefer 2½"-wide binding, but I use 2¾"-wide strips if the fabric is flannel because you need the extra width to bind the thicker flannel layers. Add the lengths of the four sides of your quilt together and add 10" more for seams and for turning the corners. Divide this number by 40 (40" of usable length from each strip) and round up to the nearest whole number. This is the number of strips you need to cut.

Cutting Bias Binding

1. Align the 45° line of a square ruler along the selvage and place a long ruler against it. Cut along the edge of the long ruler.

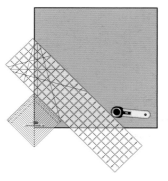

2. Align the correct measurement line on the ruler (width of the binding strip) with the previously cut edge of the fabric. Cut along the edge of the ruler. Continue cutting strips until

your ruler is not long enough to completely reach across the entire piece of fabric.

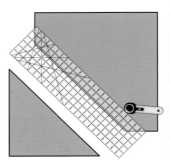

3. Carefully fold the fabric toward you as shown. Be sure the bias edges are aligned. Continue to cut the bias strips until you have enough to make the required length of the binding.

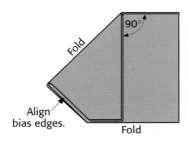

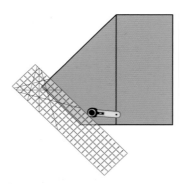

Attaching the Binding

1. With right sides together, place *straight-grain binding strips* at right angles and sew across the corner as shown. Or, with right sides together, place *bias-cut binding strips* on a diagonal and sew across the strips as shown. Trim the excess fabric, including the selvages, and press the seams open. Continue joining the

strips in this manner until you have one long strip of binding.

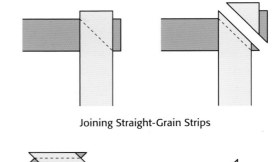

Joining Straight-Grain Strips

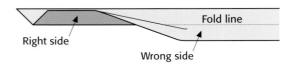

Joining Bias-Cut Strips

2. Press the long strip in half lengthwise, wrong sides together.

Right side

Wrong side

Fold line

3. Trim the batting and backing even with the edges of the quilt top. Now is the time to add a hanging sleeve if you need one. See "Adding a Hanging Sleeve" on page 89 for instructions.

4. Use a walking foot and a slightly longer stitch to sew the binding to the quilt. Align the raw edges of the binding strip with the front edge of the quilt top and start sewing near the middle of one side of the quilt, using a ¼" seam allowance. Leave at least the first 6" of the binding strip unsewn so it will be free for finishing the binding at the end. Stop sewing ¼" from the corner of the quilt.

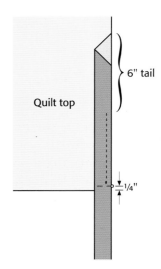

6" tail

Quilt top

¼"

5. Remove the needle from the quilt and turn the quilt so you will be sewing down the next side. Fold the binding up, away from the quilt, with raw edges aligned. Fold the binding back down onto itself, even with the edge of the quilt top. Start sewing ¼" from the corner and backstitch. Continue sewing down this side of the quilt. Repeat this process on the remaining corners and sides of the quilt.

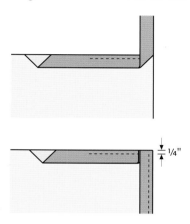

6. When you are again sewing on the side where you started, stop sewing approximately 7" from where you began. Overlap the beginning tail with the ending tail. Trim the binding tails with a straight cut so the overlap is exactly the same distance as the width of your binding strips. (If your binding strips are 2½" wide, the overlap should be 2½"; for 2¾"-wide binding, the overlap should be 2¾".)

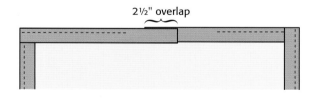

7. Unfold the two ends of the binding and place the tails right sides together so they form a right angle as shown. Draw a diagonal line from corner to corner and pin the strips together.

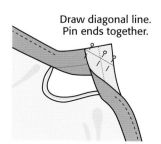

Draw diagonal line. Pin ends together.

8. Sew along the diagonal line, trim the seam allowance to ¼", and press the seam open. Refold the binding and press. Align the raw edges of the binding with the edge of the quilt top and finish sewing. Start sewing ½" back into the previous stitching and continue sewing ½" past the stitching at the beginning.

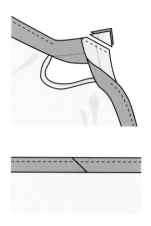

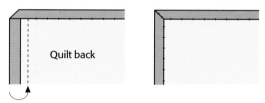

9. Turn the binding to the back of the quilt to cover the machine stitching line. Hand sew the binding in place, mitering the corners when you come to them.

Quilt back

Signing Your Quilt

Many people will see your quilt in the years to come and want to know all about it. Make a label to attach to the back of your quilt that gives your name (first, middle, maiden, last), the city and state where you lived when you made the quilt, and the date you finished. If someone else did the quilting or some other part of the quilt, give his or her name, city, and state as well. Does this quilt have a name? Was it given to someone as a gift, and for what occasion? Was it made for a special purpose? These are all things you can add to your label. When the information is complete, turn the raw edges under and blindstitch the label to the back of your quilt.

Bibliography

Brackman, Barbara. *Encyclopedia of Pieced Quilt Patterns.* Paducah, Ky: American Quilter's Society, 1993; originally published by Prairie Flower Publishing, 1984.

Gordon, Maggi McCormick. *1000 Great Quilt Blocks.* Woodinville, Wash.: Martingale & Company, 2003.

Hopkins, Judy. *Around the Block with Judy Hopkins: 200 Rotary-Cut Blocks in 6 Sizes.* Woodinville, Wash.: Martingale & Company, 1994.

———. *Around the Block Again: More Rotary-Cut Blocks from Judy Hopkins.* Woodinville, Wash.: Martingale & Company, 2000.

———. *Once More Around the Block.* Woodinville, Wash.: Martingale & Company, 2003.

Hopkins, Judy, and Nancy J. Martin. *101 Fabulous Rotary-Cut Quilts.* Woodinville, Wash.: Martingale & Company, 1998.

Martin, Nancy J. *365 Quilt Blocks a Year: Perpetual Calendar.* Woodinville, Wash.: Martingale & Company, 1999.

About the Author

Laurie Bevan's passion is quiltmaking. She was "bitten by the bug" in 1992, thanks to her good friends Laura and Suzanne who took her on her first visit to a quilt shop and shared with her the fun of quilting. She hasn't stopped since.

Every year, like migrating birds, Laurie and her friends head south to Sisters, Oregon, for the annual outdoor quilt show. They spend an entire week together, quilting, shopping, and attending classes and lectures. On Saturday, 1000 quilts are displayed all over the town hanging on the outside of buildings. Laurie's favorite part of the trip, however, is spending seven days together with her good friends and all the other quilters she meets each year, sharing their lives and their love of quilting.

Laurie was a major contributor to the book *Triangle Tricks* (Martingale & Company, 2003) and is very proud of its success. She is currently a freelance technical editor for Martingale & Company and says it's fun to work on other authors' books as well as her own.

From the quilting studio in her home on the Hood Canal in Washington State, Laurie enjoys designing and sewing, sometimes reading or knitting, but always watching the beautiful changing scenery outside her window.

New and Bestselling Titles from

Martingale & COMPANY

America's Best-Loved Craft & Hobby Books®
America's Best-Loved Knitting Books®

That Patchwork Place®

America's Best-Loved Quilt Books®

NEW RELEASES
300 Paper-Pieced Quilt Blocks
American Doll Quilts
Classic Crocheted Vests
Dazzling Knits
Follow-the-Line Quilting Designs
Growing Up with Quilts
Hooked on Triangles
Knitting with Hand-Dyed Yarns
Lavish Lace
Layer by Layer
Lickety-Split Quilts
Magic of Quiltmaking, The
More Nickel Quilts
More Reversible Quilts
No-Sweat Flannel Quilts
One-of-a-Kind Quilt Labels
Patchwork Showcase
Pieced to Fit
Pillow Party!
Pursenalities
Quilter's Bounty
Quilting with My Sister
Seasonal Quilts Using Quick Bias
Two-Block Appliqué Quilts
Ultimate Knitted Tee, The
Vintage Workshop, The
WOW! Wool-on-Wool Folk Art Quilts

APPLIQUÉ
Appliquilt in the Cabin
Blossoms in Winter
Garden Party
Shadow Appliqué
Stitch and Split Appliqué
Sunbonnet Sue All through the Year

HOLIDAY QUILTS & CRAFTS
Christmas Cats and Dogs
Christmas Delights
Hocus Pocus!
Make Room for Christmas Quilts
Welcome to the North Pole

LEARNING TO QUILT
101 Fabulous Rotary-Cut Quilts
Happy Endings, Revised Edition
Loving Stitches, Revised Edition
More Fat Quarter Quilts
Quilter's Quick Reference Guide, The
Sensational Settings, Revised Edition
Simple Joys of Quilting, The
Your First Quilt Book (or it should be!)

PAPER PIECING
40 Bright and Bold Paper-Pieced Blocks
50 Fabulous Paper-Pieced Stars
Down in the Valley
Easy Machine Paper Piecing
For the Birds
Papers for Foundation Piecing
Quilter's Ark, A
Show Me How to Paper Piece
Traditional Quilts to Paper Piece

QUILTS FOR BABIES & CHILDREN
Easy Paper-Pieced Baby Quilts
Easy Paper-Pieced Miniatures
Even More Quilts for Baby
More Quilts for Baby
Quilts for Baby
Sweet and Simple Baby Quilts

ROTARY CUTTING/SPEED PIECING
365 Quilt Blocks a Year Perpetual
   Calendar
1000 Great Quilt Blocks
Burgoyne Surrounded
Clever Quarters
Clever Quilts Encore
Endless Stars
Once More around the Block
Pairing Up
Stack a New Deck
Star-Studded Quilts
Strips and Strings
Triangle-Free Quilts

SCRAP QUILTS
Easy Stash Quilts
Nickel Quilts
Rich Traditions
Scrap Frenzy
Successful Scrap Quilts

TOPICS IN QUILTMAKING
Asian Elegance
Batiks and Beyond
Bed and Breakfast Quilts
Coffee-Time Quilts
Dutch Treat
English Cottage Quilts
Fast-Forward Your Quilting
Machine-Embroidered Quilts
Mad about Plaid!
Romantic Quilts
Simple Blessings

CRAFTS
20 Decorated Baskets
Beaded Elegance
Blissful Bath, The
Collage Cards
Creating with Paint
Holidays at Home
Pretty and Posh
Purely Primitive
Stamp in Color
Trashformations
Warm Up to Wool
Year of Cats...in Hats!, A

KNITTING & CROCHET
365 Knitting Stitches a Year Perpetual
   Calendar
Beyond Wool
Classic Knitted Vests
Crocheted Aran Sweaters
Crocheted Lace
Crocheted Socks!
Garden Stroll, A
Knit it Now!
Knits for Children and Their Teddies
Knits from the Heart
Knitted Throws and More
Knitter's Template, A
Little Box of Scarves, The
Little Box of Sweaters, The
Style at Large
Today's Crochet
Too Cute! Cotton Knits for Toddlers